M000249645

From a Small Town to the Big World

Norman Boehm

FOREWORD BY ALEKSANDRA ZIOLKOWSKA-BOEHM

For Dr. Jean H Wahl

with all my good wishes,

Aleksandra Ziolkowska-Boehm

Hamilton Books

An Imprint of
Rowman & Littlefield
Lanham • Boulder • New York • Toronto • Plymouth, UK

April 4, 2017

Copyright © 2017 by Hamilton Books
4501 Forbes Boulevard, Suite 200, Lanham, Maryland 20706
Hamilton Books Acquisitions Department (301) 459-3366

Unit A, Whitacre Mews, 26-34 Stannary Street,
London SE11 4AB, United Kingdom

All rights reserved
Printed in the United States of America
British Library Cataloguing in Publication Information Available

Library of Congress Control Number: 2016957273
ISBN: 978-0-7618-6876-7 (pbk : alk. paper)—ISBN: 978-0-7618-6877-4 (electronic)

∞™ The paper used in this publication meets the minimum requirements of American National Standard for Information Sciences Permanence of Paper for Printed Library Materials, ANSI/NISO Z39.48-1992.

Contents

Photographs

The following photographs appear in a gallery following page 39.

Blenda (née Bergman), Carl Adalbert Boehm, and their son Carl Norman, August 1905

Blenda with her grandson Norman, and dog "Cop" No 1

Norman with his mother Erna and father Carl Norman

Norman and "Cop" No 2

Norman as High School fire chief

Norman Graduation

Norman in Navy, 19 years old

Ingrid Bergman and Norman, Deauville, France 1956

Norman and Ingrid Bergman, London 1980

High School Reunion, Washington, NJ 1990, Norman and Aleksandra Boehm

Norman at sculpture of Crazy Horse by Korczak Ziolkowski, Crazy Horse Memorial, South Dakota 1994

I am grateful to Ana Cosenza for restoring old photos in this collection

Foreword
by Aleksandra Ziolkowska-Boehm

I did not know that my husband's memoirs would be published after his death. [1]
I did not know that I would write the foreword. . . . Like all of us . . . I did not
know many things . . . .

Norman was an extraordinary man. I was always charmed by his unique
character traits, such as tact and modesty. I would like to share some of my
memories about my husband, especially what kind of person he was for me
as well as for others.

Ingrid Bergman beautifully described him - then 20-something years old -
after their meeting in Paris. In my book "Ingrid Bergman and her American
Relatives", I quoted the letter of the great actress which she wrote about
Norman to his father.

> *My Dear Cousin—(. . .) I doubt that I wrote you after your son was here. I*
> *remember we sent you a card together, but I wanted to write you again without*
> *Norman knowing it, to tell you he is wonderful! What a pleasure when one can*
> *be so proud of a child as you have all the right to be. He is simple, gracious,*
> *undemanding (these are qualities that Americans in Europe not very often*
> *have!). He is intelligent, and clean. Well, I mean his soul is clean!! I really*
> *wish him all the happiness possible. I think he has done well taking this job far*
> *away, so he can get some money and a good position, even if right now it's a*
> *little tough on a young man.(. . .)* [2]

As I wrote in my book - What beautiful words about Norman were written by such a wonderful lady . . . I can only state, that the Norman I met and
married, was the same: gracious, undemanding, intelligent and very much a
gentleman. He was like the characters played by Jimmy Stewart.

My beloved husband is present in a few of my books: "Ingrid Bergman and Her American Relatives", "On the Road with Suzy From Cat to Companion", "Open Wounds—A Native American Heritage", "Love for Family, Friends, and Books".

We were proud of each other. It was precious and important to me that Norman seeing how much time I spent writing, he was not irritated, nor did he ever make sarcastic remarks. On the contrary - he was warm and encouraging. When I was writing my book "Open Wounds—A Native American Heritage" he became deeply interested in and sympathetic to the plight of Native Americans, he supported Indian schools and charitable organizations. Without his emotional and intellectual engagement I would not have been able to present an important voice on this difficult American issue, which received great acclaim and reviews, both in Poland and America.

Norman was reserved, attentive and had respect for other people, other cultures and religions. It beautifully matched in our marriage. I was born, raised and educated in Poland, and I felt a great appreciation for his attitude towards otherness. He showed me how he enjoyed getting to know the people, customs and history of my country. Through the years Norman appealed to the US media many times, pointing out lies and false accusations regarding Polish issues. He did it himself, with his own sensibility. He engaged in the effort of Poland's ultimately successful accession to NATO.[3] He initiated sending letters to US congressmen and corresponded on this issue with then Senator Joe Biden and Senator Kay Bailey Hutchinson.

Norman and I were both mature to know what a treasure it is to meet another person whom you admire, respect and love. Each day was important, because we were together. We became good friends; we talked a lot– about our joys, hopes and fears. We never hurt each other's feelings. We exchanged hundreds of notes, love letters, and wrote short poems to each other. I encouraged him to write his memoirs for quite a long time. He wrote slowly, showing me excerpts along the way. He completed the whole book a month before his death.

Norman was a wonderful talented man with a gentle and sensitive soul. He loved music and played the piano beautifully. His love, devotion, fairness and kindness were great gifts from God. I am very grateful to have been his wife for 26 years. He appreciated and did not take for granted any of the good things he received from others. Our years of being together were the most beautiful and special ones for me. He made my life complete.

Norman in his memoirs does not write about his private life - by choice. He raised, by himself three children: Erik, Kara and Kurt. Below I quote the statements about their father, and also thoughts of his stepson, my son Thomas.

Erik:

It is often said we choose our friends but not our family, however, I feel as though I chose my Father that I decided to be his son. He was a mentor, friend, confidant, and guide throughout my life leading me to choices that made me a better person. I will miss the times he gave me a word of advice, a suggestion, a thought, an insight, but will always remember and cherish them. He gave wonderful gifts that showed me he understood me in a way no one else did, for example, a baseball bat on my tenth birthday or a painting of my dog Hokey not long after he passed away. I thank God I chose him to be my Father for all I learned and came to value from his life.

Kara:

He was the best dad a little girl could ask for. Strict but hands on, my dad parented with a perfect blend of discipline and love. He devoted his free time to his kids, and in turn, we developed many common interests including playing piano, skiing, swimming, travel, and a love for animals. When he became a single dad, he worked hard to make a difficult situation the best it could be for me. He always had a way of making me feel special and through his words and actions, he taught me to work hard, be responsible, and enjoy life. My dad was a perfect gentleman—intelligent, kind, responsible, and generous. But more importantly, he was the person who influenced my life most and the best dad a girl could ask for.

Kurt:

My Father is the finest example of a man that I could ever have wished for. He raised his children on his own for many years, working full time, ensuring his children's lives were wonderful and good, without a complaint. I witnessed his faith in God many times, often sitting at the edge of his bed in prayer. When I was disciplined, within an hour he was forgiving me and offering encouragement. I am extremely fortunate to have been born into this world to such a fine Father, caring provider, mentor and friend, who will live in my heart, always. I wish I could be as great a man; he set the mark so high in his example. I would be very fortunate if I left such an impact on my children.

My son, Thomas Tomczyk, shared his thoughts:

I used to think of Norman as my stepfather and it took me 25 years to realize he was really my dad. Norman for all these years offered me his guidance, his advice and calmed me down with his patience. He was encouraging even when I doubted myself. He was unconditionally supportive when I needed help. He had words of wisdom when I was lost for words.

He was a planer that was both realistic and pragmatic. With these qualities life path led him to do amazing things in amazing places.

His one fear was to become a burden to others and he never did. Even in his last days Norman taught me the value of family, perseverance, patience. He gave me an example I hope to follow my entire life.

Norman's memoirs are shown without any changes, the way he completed them.

They are—in my opinion—captivating, interesting and showing us how to go through life with honesty and curiosity.

My husband had the distinctive gift of winning people over. He had acquaintances and friendships with many interesting people who reciprocated his extraordinary kindness and warmth. Below are a few examples:

Over the years I had the pleasure of conversing with Norman on a variety of topics we both found interesting, and even some that I didn't know I had an interest in until Norm brought them to life. Norm had this impressive ability to stitch together many separate and distinct conversations from the one at hand, and tie them all back together to form the fabric for another opportunity to better understand the world we live and navigate in. Norm was worldly, well-traveled, and deeply informed in a number of subject areas. Yet in all his wisdom and knowledge, he was above all else, kind, caring, non-judgmental and an appreciative soul, of the world, its inhabitants, and the cultures they express. In particular his keen interest in Native American cultures of the Northern Plains Tribes was filled with compassion, admiration, and respect for our people and our dedication to maintaining our cultural values in this fast changing world.

Rodney Trahan
Member of the Northern Cheyenne Tribe, Board Member for Partnership with Native Americans

The smorgasbord of Norman Boehm's life experiences enthralled me. Whether it was his compassion for Native Americans or Arabs and respect for other cultures and faiths, or him learning the "Jitterbug", to his close relationship with Ingrid Bergman, there is a plethora of evidence of a life full of passion and well lived! The book is sprinkled with numerous anecdotes and "pearls" of wisdom for the discerning reader. As his personal physician for over a decade I was privileged to see his stoicism and grit in the face of failing health.

He led a life I believe "worth emulating.

Vinod Kripalu, M.D.

Member of Delaware Medical Relief team (which responded to earthquakes in Haiti and Nepal) and Premiere Charities (which serve the homeless of Wilmington and an orphanage in India)

I have known Norman for many years; we met when he came to the bookstore I manage, and asked me for a particular item which was not available in the city. I told him that I would try to get it for him, took his telephone number and promised to call him when I had the item. It took about four months and a trip to Lebanon, where I found the item and brought it back. I called him thinking that he might have forgotten. But he showed up the following day and thanked me for my efforts. That was the beginning of our friendship. We talked a lot about Lebanon and life in Saudi Arabia in the sixties, and of course, every now and then we delved into political discussions. Norman was a real 'Gentleman' with a capital 'G'. Throughout the years, though he might disagree with something I said, he would look at me and say, "You might be right."

A few weeks before he passed away, he told me an episode that took place during his first week in Lebanon. He said, "I will never forget the taste of Laziza. I still can feel the taste." So, while I was in Lebanon, I brought him back a bottle of Laziza beer and sent it by mail to him. He called a couple of days later to thank me in a way that made me feel unworthy of his friendship.

Issam T. Masri

Publisher and Book Distributor

We cross paths with an infinite number of people in our lives but find few who are able to energize our souls. Norman Boehm was one of those few who was a cavern of unexplored chambers each filled with richness and discovery. I first met Norman in a doctor-patient relationship. He appeared to be a wise, informed and intuitive person who could understand and verbalize his own medical conditions. But I soon learned that the depth of his knowledge and interests would take me decades to explore.

We first discussed his work in the Arabian Peninsula and his understanding of the Israeli-Palestinian conflict. He saw firsthand the inequities in the situation and the violation of human rights against the Palestinians. Little did I know that he had numerous other expeditions in life that included Native Americans and forgotten peoples everywhere. Each conversation was not only enriching but provided an image of a deeply motivated and compassionate individual. Besides having meetings with Norman and Aleksandra, I would occasionally call Norman just to have conversations; I seek his opin-

ions on a variety of subjects. His patience, compassion and depth of knowledge made him the penultimate teacher. And even at his funeral service I was surprised to learn even more of the many facets of this wise soul.

It was a privilege to be able to share in his care but even more so to be called a friend. He has given so much to so many without ever requiring recognition. Norman truly made the world a better place without asking anything in return.

Robert Abel Jr., M.D.
Ophthalmologist, Educator, Author

NOTES

1. Norman Boehm passed away on May 26, 2016.
2. To: Carl Norman Boehm, Wyoming, Pennsylvania, Paris, Hotel Raphael, December 14, 1955. The whole letter: Aleksandra Ziolkowska-Boehm, "Ingrid Bergman and Her American Relatives", Hamilton Books, 2013, pp. 54-55.
3. It is posted in Jan Nowak–Jezioranski "The Polish Road to NATO", Wroclaw 2006.

Preface

Since our marriage in 1990, my wife Aleksandra often suggested that I write a story of my life. My response was always that I had not lived a very exciting life worth writing about. Her counter argument was that I did have an exciting and eventful life, and one that I could be proud of. In Poland in 2007 with Aleksandra as she fulfilled a Fulbright research scholarship, I received a letter from my daughter Kara suggesting I write about my life. Her suggestion was based upon the fact that time and distance had eroded any relationships with her four sons then of ages 15, 13, 8 and 4. She believed that my story would be of interest to them as they would learn a bit about their living grandfather. Considering Aleksandra's and Kara's similar ideas, I started to give some thought to such a writing project. Concluding that a chronological resume would be boring and not interesting to anyone, I decided that I would write of events in my life that "stood out" in my memory. Some of these events were exciting, some were embarrassing, some were happy, some were sad, some were failures, some were achievements, but most importantly, they should be, in my opinion, of interest to potential readers. I began my writing project on 18 July 2007. What follows are events in my life (not in chronological order) that occurred during boyhood years, grade school years, high school years, university years and through manhood until marriage.

I have purposely excluded personal events that I believe do not belong in this type of story. Also, having been named after my father Carl Norman Boehm, I became Carl Norman Boehm Jr. For the purposes of my story, I will only identify myself as Norman Boehm.

Growing up in the small New Jersey town of Washington, my parents were well aware of the frequent high school romances of young couples maturing into marriages after graduation. My father was particularly concerned of such events and regularly advised me not to become over involved with a girl friend. He did not want a romance to deter me from pursuing a college education in engineering, and I was receptive to his advice. On completion of high school, his influence led me to enter the University of North Dakota (UND) in Grand Forks. The university had been highly recommended to him by a graduate of the school and a colleague during his war time employment with the New York Shipbuilding Corporation in Camden, NJ.

My first venture away from home was a 1600 mile bus journey to North Dakota in September 1945. This also achieved another piece of advice from my father: to separate me from "my mother's apron strings" and to mature accordingly.

After graduation from UND with a degree in chemical engineering, I found employment with the Wyandotte Chemicals Corporation in Wyandotte, Michigan doing organic chemical research that I did not find fulfilling. However, from a colleague, I learned about the Arabian American Oil Company (Aramco) in Saudi Arabia and its employment opportunities. Granted an interview by Aramco, I was offered employment in its New York City offices for an approximate 20 month period to be followed by transfer to the company's Ras Tanura Refinery as a process engineer. I opted to think about the offer but actually wanted to seek my father's advice once again. His advice was short and to the point: "If you don't take that opportunity you're nuts". So, I accepted Aramco's job offer.

Norman in Zelazowa Wola, Poland, the birth place of Frederic Chopin

My second venture away was to New York City in October 1952 and subsequently to Saudi Arabia in June of 1954. Thus began my lifetime adventure with travel twice around the world, countries of Asia and the Middle East, Europe, England, Norway, Poland and many locations in the USA.

Chapter One

My German and Swedish Ancestry

Mention of my paternal grandparents Carl Adalbert Heinrich and Blenda Helena Boehm is important for me. Both were immigrants to the U.S. before 1900, as my father was born that year in Chicago after they met and married. Carl immigrated from Bad Kissingen in Bavaria of Germany, Blenda immigrated from Slattog, Sweden, and both became U.S. citizens. Blenda's brother Justus married a German woman named Friedel Adler, and their only daughter was the famous actress Ingrid Bergman. Ingrid was always considered as Swedish by the media with no mention that she was half German since her mother was born in Germany. Following the birth of my father (16 November 1900), my grandmother began to suffer from a creeping paralysis that started in her feet and gradually crept up her body such that it made her an invalid for the last twenty-five years of her life. Always hopeful that she would walk again, it never happened. She was a heavy burden for my grandfather and my father who often had to carry her here and there, for example, from the house to the car.

Following the demise of the shade manufacturing business, my grandparents moved to an area near Athens, Georgia in the Smokey Mountains. They were hopeful that a better climate with clean air would benefit my grandmother, and they wanted to be near friends from the "Laymen's Home Missionary Movement", a Christian bible study group. Being an invalid for so many years, my grandmother became an astute bible student but at the same time tried to impose her beliefs too often. To this my father rebelled, and he never pushed me, nor would he cooperate with the Presbyterian Church where as a boy I attended Sunday school, when at twelve years of age, they endeavored to have me join the church. He believed that I could make my own decision on what church to join, and I did so at the age of twenty-eight joining the Wyoming Presbyterian Church in Wyoming, Pennsylvania where my father and his second wife Marien were members.

My grandfather always encouraged me to go to college and would award me with one dollar on occasion for a good report card. My father always deeply regretted not finishing his study of mechanical engineering at the Stevens Institute of Technology (in Hoboken, New Jersey) because of interest in a girl friend. He too always encouraged me to work and do well in school. His encouragement was also based upon his own experience to not become too involved with girls at an early age such that they detracted from the prime goal of a college education. My grandfather's last word to my Dad was "Good" on learning at his death-bed that I was going to attend the University of North Dakota (UND). My mother wanted me to be at home and attend Lafayette College in nearby Easton, Pennsylvania (fifteen miles from Washington). However, here again, my Dad prevailed. He chose the North Dakota university to move me away – as I wrote earlier - from my mother's "apron strings" (a very wise move I came to realize), as well as to attend a very fine engineering school. UND had been recommended to my father by a colleague and graduate of the school. They met at the New York Shipbuilding Corporation in Camden, New Jersey where my father worked during the latter part of the war years. The colleague proclaimed that "If your son completes one year there, he will want to finish there", and it came true.

Mention of my maternal grandparents Richard and Selma Sehm is also very important for me. Both were German immigrants from Thalheim, a suburb of Chemnitz in the Saxony region of Germany. Richard was responsible for maintenance of silk hosiery weaving machinery made in Germany and installed in a hosiery mill in Dover, New Jersey. He came to the U.S. several years before my grandmother and family, and like many such people worked to accumulate enough money to bring his family. He accomplished this. My mother remembers at the age of ten years being on the last ship from Germany to the U.S. before America entered World War I. She recalls the voyage was made with portholes closed and blacked out at night to avoid attracting German submarines and possible torpedo attacks.

Arriving in 1917, my mother was thrown into grade school, not able to speak English, and taunted with words such as "Kraut", "Heinie" etc. She survived all this, finished grade school and later became a U.S. citizen. Neither of my maternal grandparents learned English. Neither became citizens. My mother was the youngest of twelve children. Two sons were killed in World War I, others died at childbirth such that my mother and her siblings, Uncle Max, Aunt Elsie and Aunt Frieda only survived to come to the U.S. My mother lost her German accent, however, her siblings were all conversant in English with heavy accents. Although not able to speak English, my grandmother exuded love, warmth and hospitality. It was wonderful to visit her, eat the good German cooking, to enjoy something you no longer

Norman with his wife Aleksandra and his Mother Erna

find…hard crusted "Kaiser" rolls which she obtained from a local bakery catering to a large population of German speaking people. At that time, Dover consisted primarily of Italian and German ancestry people. Here I will relate what I consider to be one failure of my life. I never learned to speak German, and although I like to use the excuse that my mother could have taught me the language at home, it was up to me. I should have done so when I was young if only so I could talk to my grandparents. When I entered high school, I was hopeful of studying German, however, because we were at war with Germany, the state of New Jersey (like many others) dumbly decided to cease the teaching of German. Therefore, I had to elect another language, and I chose Spanish that I studied for two years.

Chapter Two

Boyhood and Grade School Years

Born in Dover, New Jersey in the home of my maternal grandparents on Sunday 12 February 1928 during a heavy snowstorm, perhaps it was a premonition of later years and love of winter and winter sports. About two years later, my parents Erna and Norman moved with me to Washington, New Jersey, so that my father could work for my grandfather Carl at his Woodweb Shade Manufacturing Company. As a small manufacturing plant that I remember well, looms imported from Germany were used to weave window shades from wooden "staves". The concept of wooden shades initially was very successful, however, the 1929 stock market failure and subsequent depression years that followed decimated many small businesses including that of my grandfather. The concept has continued to this day, and similar wooden shades are often seen in many homes of stylish decor.

As a boy, I grew up in a two bedroom bungalow type home on Park Hill Road on the outskirts of Washington. For a period of time, my grandparents Blenda and Carl Boehm lived in another two bedroom bungalow type home diagonally across Park Hill Road from us. A few years later, my grandparents moved to Georgia, and my mother, father and I moved into their house.

COWBOYS AND INDIANS

As a little boy I wanted to be an "Indian", and the game of "Cowboys and Indians" was a game often played with neighborhood boy friends. My first cowboy hero from the movies was Ken Maynard, a handsome western hero with sleek black hair and a beautiful white horse. Ken Maynard made a personal stage appearance in the Washington movie theater with his horse, and my friends and I were very excited to be able to see this real life hero. When he came onto the stage drunk and clumsily falling over himself, I

5

became very disenchanted with him and other cowboy heroes, perhaps thinking they were probably all the same. Subsequently, in the game of "Cowboys and Indians", my preference was to be an Indian even more because I started to feel compassion for them as they were always portrayed as losers in the movies. As history reveals, sometimes the Indians won.

To this day, I am very compassionate for them because of the mistreatment, cruelty and indifference they have suffered by the U.S. Government throughout American history. There was a heavily wooded area probably 2000 feet or so from our house at a higher elevation, and within these woods, nature had left a huge single boulder perhaps 15 feet high and 20 feet or so wide. The rock could be climbed, and it afforded a great lookout location for more "Cowboys and Indians". My friends and I named it "Indian Rock".

SECOND AMBITION–BASEBALL

My other dream as a little boy was to be a professional baseball player. The rural area of Washington, New Jersey in Warren County was one of much interest in sports as are many rural areas, and baseball was of great interest to its people. My father started me throwing a baseball at the age of five, and I still remember awaiting his return from work in the summer. As soon as he opened the front door, I would say "Let's have a catch, Dad". I do not recall

First Row, Left to Right—Pete Perini, Mike Fucci, Captain Reno Guidi, Nick Fiore, Jack Julian, Jerry Blanche, Earl Mattison, Kenneth Lobb, Dominic Fucci. *Second Row* — Duane Alpaugh, Fred Hahn, Berker Boyer, Alfred Singley, Mr. Steinhardt, Coach; Russell Riegel, Walter Bolmer, Duane Bath, Albert DeCresci. *Third Row*—Robert Wallace, Howard Tice, Norman Boehm, James Lawyer, Walter Worrall, Neal Mowder, Manager.

1944 Baseball Team

him ever turning down my request, and perhaps it was his early support that led to my being a very good fielder. My interest in baseball "took off" at the age of six when my Dad took me to the old Polo Grounds in New York City to see the New York Giants play the St. Louis Cardinals. Both teams were loaded with talent of Hall of Fame quality, such as Bill Terry, Mel Ott, Carl Hubbell of the Giants and Dizzy Dean, Joe Medwick, and Pepper Martin of the Cardinals.

In 1934 (I was then 6 years old) for this outing, my Dad had invited a friend named Bill Zitsman, who had been a major league player and who knew the players of both teams. Before the game started, Bill Zitsman went down into the dugouts of both teams to say hello to the players, and he returned with a scorecard autographed by all of the above players and others. Needless to say, I cherished this scorecard for years and kept it in a scrapbook with a collection of pictures of major league players. Somehow, after I went off to college, my wonderful scrapbook with scorecard disappeared along with other possessions (I will write about them later).

The next year, at age seven, my Dad took me to the old Yankee Stadium (the so called house that Babe Ruth built) in New York City to see the Yankees. In the one year, somehow I had become a Yankee fan and was enamored with the great Lou Gehrig. To see him and the other Yankee players such as Frankie Crosetti, Bill Dickey, Tommy Henrich, Red Ruffing, Lefty Gomez, and others, was my greatest thrill of that time. Lou Gehrig remained my favorite player until his career was ended by the paralysis disease that was later named after him. He was followed by Bill Dickey and then Joe DiMaggio, all my favorites now being in the Hall of Fame.

Summer activities for young boys like me were mainly comprised of playing baseball in the morning and swimming in the afternoon at the town park which provided a baseball field, tennis courts and a pool. The baseball game was started by the oldest two boys choosing up sides, and the game was played without any uniforms or support of our parents. We just wanted to play baseball, and we did this almost everyday except when it rained. Tennis was not too popular for the boys, some even considering it a "sissy" sport which was a ridiculous judgment of it. So I did learn the game and did play it on occasion. Then in the afternoon, my friends and I would swim in the pool, not for a short time but all afternoon.

The love of swimming I have to credit my parents for. As a two year old, they took me into the water, and I would hang onto my father's back as he swam and my mother would swim alongside just in case I lost my hold around his neck. These swimming ventures usually took place on weekends at nearby Mountain Lake, a small spring-fed lake about three-fourths of a mile wide, one mile long but very deep, located seven miles from Washington. They continued until I went off to college. Quite often in the summer, my parents would rent a cottage at the lake for a week's period, so we did a

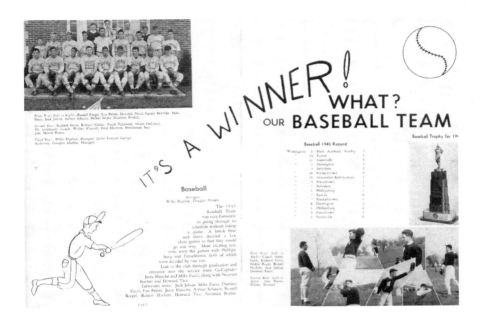

1945 Baseball Team

lot of swimming and sometimes fishing. I know I made my father very proud, when at the age of nine, I swam across Mountain Lake non-stop and free style (then defined as the Australian crawl) for a distance of three-fourths of a mile. I was not alone as he accompanied me in a canoe just in case I floundered. Another event for me was my first dive from a twenty feet high tower at the lake. Never did I fear jumping from the height, but diving was a more fearful challenge. I guess I finally made the dive at ten or eleven years . . . it took time for me to build up my courage!

WINTER SPORTS

Winter sports in the North Jersey town are wonderful to recall. We lived on Park Hill Road outside of town and on a modest sized hill. Snow brought us the opportunity to sleigh ride when the snow packed on the road. The hill permitted a ride of about 300 yards (it seemed longer then), and at the bottom of the hill, there was the option of a left turn or to go straight for another 100 yards in either direction. The left turn was often difficult to make, and on one occasion a friend and I sledding together crashed into a car parked on the curve and suffered sore heads for a few days. We also had open fields about a half-mile away with modest slopes, so we skied using the old-fashioned skis with a strap across the foot (no boots so you could turn the skis). These skis limited you to going straight only and to stopping by falling down. To make our skiing more of a challenge, we constructed ski jumps by building up the snow to three feet or so, making a straight line track to the jump and then thrilling to the elevation our efforts afforded. More often than not, lifting off the jump was a disaster because it was difficult to keep the skis straight with their single strap construction. But it was great fun. In the winter of 1939, which was particularly severe, we experienced a snowfall of about thirty inches followed by a cold spell with temperatures below freezing even in the daytime. The result of this cold spell was sleigh riding on Park Hill Road and skiing the open fields behind our house for six weeks. The snow became thickly crusted from the freezing temperatures, and it was amazing to us that we were able to walk on top of the snow and be able to sled on top of the crust. In addition, Mountain Lake froze over completely such that there was ice skating for six weeks as well. I was never very talented as an ice skater, and I had a real problem with weak ankles such that I could not keep my ankles straight (a requisite for skating). On the other hand, my father was a beautiful skater who could skate equally well backwards or forwards, and he would support me as I endeavored to accomplish this sport. As a sideline, it was not until many years later when I worked in New York City that I took up ice skating again at the age of twenty-two. After a winter of skating at the Wollman Memorial outdoor rink in Central Park, I managed to strengthen my ankles such that I no longer needed support straps to keep them straight, but I never accomplished the ability to skate backwards.

MY FIRST AIRPLANE RIDE

The first great thrill of my youth had to be when, at the age of six years, my father enticed me into my first airplane ride. Another of his friends named Ford Slacker was a pilot who flew airplane rides for paying customers during the summer fair season. I used the word "enticed", because I was not immediately excited about an airplane ride in a single-engine aircraft, but I do not recall its model. Actually, I was afraid to go, but my Dad finally managed to convince me that I would love it. And love it I did! I hated to see the ride end. Here again, I must credit my father for instilling in me a life long interest and love for flying such that years later, I obtained my single-engine pilots license, one of my greatest achievements. But immediately after the airplane ride, I began to enjoy the fun of building model airplanes. My preference was the type of models that require the builder to construct of balsam wood the framework for the fuselage, the wings, the elevators and the rudder. This was slow, tedious work as the construction had to comply with a special drawing showing all members that had to be "pinned" together and then glued. Next, a rubber elastic band was fastened from the rear of the fuselage to the balsam propeller at the engine front of the plane. Finally, when the framework of the various aircraft sections was completed, they were joined and covered by bright colored tissue paper, also a tedious job. By rotating the propeller and winding the rubber band, the plane was ready for flight driven by the spinning propeller. Usually the plane would be airborne for a few moments and then crash. After a few such experiences, I elected to hang my finished models from the ceiling of my bedroom rather than waste all the effort of their construction to one disastrous flight.

PIANO LESSONS

At nine years of age, another interest came into my young life. My parents offered to let me take piano lessons. I agreed, but we had to have a piano. A second-hand "upright" was found and purchased for $25. My parents logically decided that it would be foolish to buy an expensive piano, when I might not take to the regimen of lessons or have any talent at all. The lessons were given by a local piano teacher named Ruth Weller, a spinster, and once per week, I would have a lesson of classical music in her home. Her piano fingers amazed me . . . from years of playing the piano, the ends of her fingers developed a swollen or knob-like appearance. I have never seen since then any pianist with such a finger condition. After about two years, my teacher and my parents believed that I would be responsive to the continued regimen of a weekly lesson, that I did have some talent (?) and therefore, I should have a better piano to play. Searching for a quality piano, my parents learned of one from my mother's nephew Bill Uhlig who lived in Hatboro, Pennsylvania. One of his neighbors, a retired opera singer had been widowed, was moving to Florida, and she had a Lester baby grand piano perhaps fifteen years old that she was selling. My parents purchased the Lester piano for $250, and that was a lot of money in those days (especially for them). The piano had been well-used . . . the red mahogany wood was in need of refinishing, but the tonal quality of the piano was unsurpassed. My father's first step was to have the piano tuned by a local tuner named John Dolan, who had been blinded as a young boy from a friend throwing sand in his eyes. John Dolan used no mechanical or electronic tuning devices (they did not exist in 1939). He tuned using his magnificent ear for and sense of tone only. Indeed, although handicapped by blindness, God had blessed him with remarkable hearing and an ear for sound. His assistant, whose name I cannot remember, was a master wood craftsman, and he completely refinished the red mahogany Lester. What the tuning and refinishing cost my Mom and Dad, I have no idea, but it must have been a "pretty penny" as well and another great sacrifice all for me. The piano was absolutely beautiful, and it had to be my most valuable possession. My piano lessons from Miss Weller continued until I reached sixteen years of age, when I decided (very stupidly looking back at this time) that I had other priorities such as sports, studies, etc. (but not girls). I am sure my parents were heartbroken, because I did have the ability to read music (but not play by ear). I had progressed to where I was playing Chopin, Beethoven, Schubert, Tchaikovsky and the like, not their most complex and difficult compositions, but certainly simplified versions of their more-famous ones. One of the highlights of my piano career was to perform a solo of Chopin's "Minute Waltz" (it probably took me more than a minute) at a concert by Miss Weller's students. I remember being extremely nervous, having to make a second start of my solo, but in the end doing the waltz quite well.

Having to practice the piano was not always something I wanted to do, but my parents laid down the rule that one hour a day was the minimum amount of practice time. Often practice was enjoyable for me particularly in the summertime. Then, with the windows open for cooling (air conditioning did not exist at that time), as I played music, I found myself in a duet with a family of wrens living in a wild cherry tree close to our house. They habitually would sing along with me in perfect harmony creating a very enjoyable performance of music provided I made no mistakes. The wrens are known to be beautiful singers, and to ensure the family would return, my father and I built two wren houses for them. The houses had to be built with the entrance port no larger than 3/4 of an inch in diameter to restrict larger birds from entering the wren house. Installed in the cherry tree, our construction effort paid off as we always had the beautiful little singers nearby.

I took 8 years of lessons and have always wished it had been longer. Now retired and more than ever before, I appreciate my ability to play the piano and thereby entertain myself and my wife. I enjoy playing the music I prefer that includes some of the more well-known classics, big band music and Latin rhythms.

After leaving for college in September 1945, my parents moved to Wilmington, Delaware as my father had obtained employment with DuPont in their Engineering Department. For them, the Lester became too much of a financial burden to transport plus I was at home no longer. Consequently, they sold the piano, the news of which I learned with sadness, however, they had sacrificed considerably to provide me with this beautiful instrument as well as the cost of lessons over nearly eight years. So I knew I had no right to question their decision to sell my piano. In this move, another cherished possession disappeared. I had been given a beautiful Columbia bicycle for Christmas at the age of eight, and it was considered the highest quality bicycle made in those days with a "coaster" brake, not a hand operated brake. I used the bicycle regularly until I went off to college. Again, I accepted my parent's decision to sell it.

MEETING INGRID BERGMAN

My piano career also included a performance for the famous actress Ingrid Bergman who visited my parents and paternal grandparents for a weekend on her first visit to the U.S. (circa 1940). My father brought her from New York City by auto to Washington with her daughter Pia (then an infant). Again I did Chopin's "Minute Waltz" and a couple of other tunes, and she flattered me with words of applause "Bravo Bravo". I also managed to proudly introduce her to a few of my neighborhood friends.

CHERISHED ANIMALS

Throughout my life, animals have occupied a very special place in my heart. I had many pets as a young boy. Included were two stray dogs that my mother welcomed into our home feeling sorry for them and a few cats as well. Our favorite cat was "Whitey". His mother was an all black stray that we took in. "Whitey" and five siblings were born in the basement coal bin, and "Whitey" being black and white was the only kitten readily discernable from the coal. My father loved dogs the most and particularly German Shepherds (sometimes called police dogs because of their use by the police). I have a picture of my paternal grandmother Blenda with me at about two years of age and my parent's dog "Cop", their first German Shepherd that I have no recollection of. I am quoting my father who said: "The German Shepherd is the most noble of the dog breeds". I could not agree more, so at the age of ten or eleven, I was begging my Mom and Dad for a "police dog". They agreed to give me one, and I recall well the responsibilities I had to accept before I would have my dog. The responsibilities were: 1. Walk the dog before going to school, 2. Walk the dog after school, and 3. Walk the dog before going to bed. Well, the responsibilities were not too much of a challenge when my male dog again aptly named "Cop" was a six months old puppy needing short walks and lots of play. However, as he matured into a seventy-five pound large dog, the walking became a real challenge as his walks were extended to about one mile per event. I was a bit on the "chubby" side as a grade schooler at that time, and walking "Cop" resulted in my losing eighteen pounds the first winter of his maturity. He loved to chase my friends and me down the hill during winter sleigh riding and nip our rears with his teeth. All animals have unique qualities and habits, and the second "Cop" was no different. He could catch a soft red rubber ball thrown in an arc from 50 feet. His favorite delicacy was seedless white grapes. He elected to be the occupier of two-thirds of my single bed. He loved to walk with me to the local butcher Knight Miller, who always had a treat for him. I loved to have him accompany me through the local park when I could taunt the local bully

Lewis Gerard (son of the park superintendent) whose habit was to beat up on smaller kids like me. If he came within ten feet of me, "Cop" would show him a full set of very white teeth and a low throated growl. Needless to say, I loved "Cop", as we all did.

Sadly, although "Cop" was very affectionate to all in my family, well-trained, he turned vicious such that he would attack strangers but never my young neighborhood friends. In those days, it was not usual to give distemper inoculations to canines, and "Cop" had not been inoculated. So, my parents decided that "Cop" had to go, after being with us about three years. My mother and I were in tears with this decision, and I am sure my Dad shed some as well when "Cop" was given to an area farmer (I'll never know if this actually happened or if he was destroyed).

MY FIRST SCHOOL

Grade school took place at a small rural school in the town of Port Colden (no water nearby but the location had been part of the Morris Canal), attended by students who lived in the areas around Washington but not in the town. Students were bussed to Port Colden, took their lunches in a paper bag or lunch box, and only drinks were available at the school but not hot lunches. I never had a problem in dedicating myself to learning, and had very good grades. At one Christmas program for the parents of students, I recall my mother hearing two women seated behind her and one of them saying "Norman Boehm is the smartest student in the school", and she often proudly repeated these words to friends and acquaintances. I always read the literature assignments given by my teachers, and can recall vividly that Mark Twain's "Huckleberry Finn" and Jack London's "Call of the Wild" were my favorite books. In these early school years, mathematics and science that required solving of problems became my favorite courses, and this never changed.

Other funny things happened to me in grade school . . . maybe not so funny to my mother and father. The school introduced us to the sport of track and field for physical education, and not being a speedy runner, I concentrated on broad jump and high jump. My achievement in these events was to badly tear the knees on two pair of brand new "knickers" bought just for school, and although my mother had a chore to repair them, I was not criticized for trying my best at a sport. Formal physical training was not a real requirement in those days, so for school physical education, we played touch football in the autumn, volleyball or "end ball" inside in the winter and baseball or track and field in the spring. There was no changing of clothes for these periods. We had to play in our school clothes. I also recall an early science project in the 4th or 5th grade where I drew a large colored drawing of the operation of an oil well and its penetration through various geological strata. Perhaps this was a foreboding of my future career in the oil industry.

Another project in geography found me making an exhibit of various spices and where in the world they were found. For this exhibit, I wrote to a spice producer who graciously provided me with actual jars of perhaps thirty or so different spices they produced which I used to accompany my exhibit.

MEMORABLE CHRISTMAS TIMES

Christmas was a wonderful time for me as a young boy thanks to my Mom and Dad who were always very generous in their giving, dedication and efforts to make my Christmases memorable. Typically, our tree was decorated two to three weeks before December 25th and was not taken down until two weeks after the New Years holiday. Both my Mom and Dad loved having the tree and enjoying its aroma that permeated the house. We always had a beautiful green spruce. The tree was mounted in the center of a wooden "spool" used to wind linen that was inset into a five gallon paint pail, both the "spool" and pail from wooden shade manufacturing operations. With the pail partially packed with coal or rocks and filled with water, my father's ingenuity in his tree mounting device provided stability and kept the tree fresh throughout the holidays by regular addition of fresh water. Another highlight of Christmas time was to travel by auto to Dover to spend Christmas Eve with my maternal grandparents Richard and Selma Sehm. A traditional German dinner was always served to all the family, and it included roast goose, kartoffelglusse (potato dumplings), red cabbage and sauerkraut. Dessert included apple strudel, lebkuchen (licorice flavored ginger cookies) and stoellen (bread with citron, raisins and a powdered sugar coating). My father always proclaimed that my grandmother's sauerkraut, and then my mother's from the same recipe, was the best he ever tasted. I am always very happy when Aleksandra prepares sauerkraut for me using the same recipe from my mother (the best I have ever tasted). My love for sauerkraut must have been born in me, because I can recall "gagging" on many vegetables when I was a youngster, but never did I do so on sauerkraut, and it was the only vegetable I would partake "seconds" of. My mother was an excellent cook, and about once per week, she would serve a typically German dinner, such as, sauerbraten, knockwurst, or wienerschnitzel and always served with sauerkraut or red cabbage. Even though she always worked in the local hosiery mill to augment family finances, she managed to find time to bake bread or her favorite cherry pie (and mine as well) and to preserve wild strawberries that we picked from the fields behind our home and other fruits.

Chapter Three

High School Years

Having "skipped" the first grade, I entered my freshman first year of high school at the age of thirteen, whereas, most of my fellow students were a year older. Certainly my physical appearance was not impressive, as I was 5 feet 2 inches tall and weighed only 118 pounds. By the end of my sophomore second year of high school, I had skyrocketed to 5 feet 9 inches in height, but my weight did not follow appropriately. I weighed only 125 pounds. As a physical "stringbean", my stature was not conducive to athletic success, and although I wanted to go out for football, my father refused to approve this venture. He was concerned I would have been badly injured. However, I went out for baseball and basketball, but I did not make the basketball varsity team until my junior third year or the baseball varsity team until my fourth senior year. I lost the opportunity for a junior year letter in baseball because I broke my right wrist in gym. The outcome of this injury was a new school ruling that baseball and basketball team members were no longer required to participate in gym during their seasons. Prior to this, only football and wrestling team members were not required to take gym during their seasons, the ruling invoked by the gym teacher Frank Bennett who was also the football and wrestling coach. I remember being very proud when I received my basketball varsity letter, so proud that I begged my mother to sew the letter onto my blue sweater so I could immediately display it at the local high school "hangout" Pop Hixon's Ice Cream Parlor. My varsity letter award followed Washington High School winning the North Central Conference basketball championship of which I was a team member. After such a successful season, our team collapsed to a 4 and 16 won loss record in my senior year, and the award of my second varsity basketball letter was more of a routine nature.

Washington High School's 1945 baseball team won the New Jersey State championship for a Group 4 school. The ratings of schools then were based upon the number of students, Group 4 being the smallest with up to 500 students. The larger schools ranged to Group 1 having up to 2000 students. The coach of the team was Joe Steinhardt whose record in New Jersey high school baseball annals is unsurpassed. He led the 1945 team to a season of 16 wins and zero losses including two defeats each of Phillipsburg and Somerville, both Group 1 New Jersey schools. We also twice defeated Easton, Pennsylvania high school, a school also of up to 2000 students. I admired Joe Steinhardt's coaching ability, but he was never one who would praise a player for a good play, but would give you a "look that would kill" if you made a bad or dumb play. I recall that one afternoon my friend Art Schaare (I will write about him later) and I, for some forgotten reason, decided to skip baseball practice, and that was an unforgiveable "sin" to Joe Steinhardt. Our next game was with Frenchtown, a bigger school, and when the game began, Art and I found ourselves sitting "on the bench" as punishment (justly deserved). After about 4 or 5 innings, Frenchtown led us 1-0, and Joe finally substituted Art and me into the game. Shortly afterwards, I found myself at bat with the bases loaded, and Joe counseled me to try and hit to right field as the right fielder was pulled way over towards centerfield. Well, I managed to hit a low pitch on the outside corner of home plate to right field for a triple which cleared the bases and won the game for us 3–1. Needless to say, Joe did not congratulate me for my game winning hit, but my teammates did. Another memory for me was a game against Clinton, a Group 4 school like

The Sophomore Class

CLASS OFFICERS

President .... RUTH GRABNER
Vice President .... ROSE CUVA
Secretary .... VIRGINIA TOTH
Treasurer .... RUTH PETERSON

Library

Top Row—Left to Right—Jack Willever, Fred Hahn, Theodore Maginnis, Robert Conant, Louis Baldwin, Joe Ferri, Harry Ley.

Second Row—Left to Right—Christina Oram, Joseph Shinrock, Augustus Sinkbile, Mrs. Bowers, Donald Coleman, Norman Boehm, Marion Cochran.

Third Row—Left to Right—Florence Jamison, Edna Ronoski, Dorothy Whitesell, Jean Farley, Marilyn Wyckoff, Shirley Snyder, Anna Mae Everly, Catherine Kinney.

Fourth Row—Left to Right—Virginia Toth, Dolores Merrill, Lila Johnson, Betty Lou Castner, Mary Pulieri, Betty Bolton, Beryl Rush, Helen Foremny.

Absent—Duane Bath, R. Kingsbury, E. Hildebrant, D. Shafer.

1943 Sophmore Class

First Row, Left to Right—Jack Julian, Frank Hassemer, Morris Potter, Ralph Fiore, Fred Hahn. Second Row—Alan Bowlby, Assistant Manager; Frank Clamer, Ernest Zelbacher, Mr. Steinhardt, Norman Boehm, Jerry Blanche, Jack Simone, Manager. Lettermen—Jerry Blanche, Norman Boehm, Arthur Schaare, Ernest Zelbacher, Fred Hahn, Frank Clamer, Jack Julian, Frank Hassemer. Co-captains — Jerry Blanche and Norman Boehm. Absent—Art Schaare.

1945 Basketball Team

Washington. Their outfield was cow pasture, and trotting to an outfield position, a fielder could manage to see and thus avoid the cow "droppings", however, when chasing a fly ball, a fielder more often than not might step onto a "dropping". The left field which I played on defense had never been leveled but was graded uphill. To go deeper for a fly ball, one had to run uphill. As luck would have it, another crucial point found Clinton loading the bases with two outs. Their next batter hit a towering fly ball to deep left field, and I immediately took off after it running uphill. I finally caught up with the ball catching it with my back to the infield. Needless to say, Joe did not say "great catch" which it was, but my teammates did. I was very surprised the next day in town when a gentleman came up to me and said: "Norman, I saw the game yesterday at Clinton, and you sure made a great catch". Very pleased, I responded, "Thank you, Sir". My high school varsity season overall was a good one. I batted .290 and fielded 1.000 as the left fielder and including playing as a substitute for our injured first baseman for two games. Joe Steinhardt was also the basketball coach, but he lacked the enthusiasm he held for baseball. Whatever success his basketball teams achieved was due to team talent, but certainly not his coaching, as we were not taught any plays, encouraged to learn new shots, defensive techniques, etc.

Cenci Sets Sail.

Intra-
Mural
Basketball

First row: (left to right)—Detrick, Maginnis, DeCresci, Shrope, Riddle, Kauffman, Hahn.
Second row: (left to right)—Burd, Mgr., Kays, D. A. Burd, McGinnis, Zelbacker, Hess, Kellow, Boehm,
Robert Wendland, Coach.

"Up in the air."

1945 Intramural Basketball Team

THE U.S.A. AT WAR

Entering high school at age thirteen, I had also become a Boy Scout as did my neighborhood friends. This was 1941, the U.S. was at war against Germany, and there were occasional signs of hostility towards those of German ancestry. One of my neighborhood friends was a year older than I, of greater stature, and in fact was a bit of a "bully" towards the younger kids of the neighborhood. A group of us were returning from a Scout meeting one evening when the Bully said to me: "Norm, if I were German, I would be ashamed of it". Well, I immediately saw "red", told him I was very proud that I was German origin (as well as Swedish), and then hit him with all my strength on the bridge of his nose right between his eyes. He then fought back giving me a bloody nose, and we exchanged a few more inconsequential punches before the fight was over. My punch was the most telling one, however, because the next day the Bully had two very, very black eyes, and he suffered the extreme embarrassment of being teased by high school classmates that "little Norman" had done this to him.

In the war years, we experienced rationing of such food staples as butter, sugar, coffee, etc. Regular sources of meat diminished as well. At this time, my father had found employment as a mechanical draftsman with the New York Shipbuilding Corporation in Camden, New Jersey who constructed U. S. Navy war vessels such as battleships and others. My father told a story about the completion of the battleship USS New Jersey when after comple-

Traffic Guides

The duties of traffic guides are to keep congestion and confusion at a minimum in the halls while classes change. These guides are chosen by the Student Council from a group of volunteers.

First Row, Left to Right — Lois Borden, Fay Sarson, Ruth Grabner, Elsie Oram, Edna Ronoski, Claire Hamlen. Louise Pedano. *Second Row* — Marjorie Frey, Edith Bellini, Shirley Coleman, Grace Godfrey, Jean Borden, Olive Rabenold, Angelina Leggio. *Third Row* — Henry Whitney, Walter Worrall, Norman Boehm, Russell Riegel, Joseph LaPrino, Fred Hahn.

1945 Traffic Guides

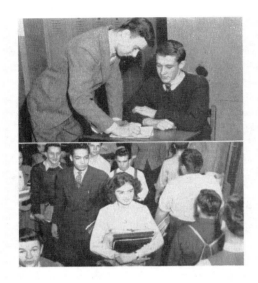

Hall Sentinels

"Sign here, please!"

Traffic Guides

"Keep moving!"

Seated, *Left to Right*—Mike Fucci, John Dellavedova, Ray Koestner, Donald Sinkway, Duane Bath, Fred Harpster. *Standing, Left to Right*—Willis Bigelow, Lewis Baldwin, Ralph Castner, Walter Worrall, Pete Perini, Robert Kingsbury, Robert Hackett. *Seated on Right*—Fred Hahn. *Demonstrator*—Norman Boehm, Fire Chief.

"Is everybody out? That's two minutes!"

FIRE CHIEF
NORMAN BOEHM

Fire Squad

Several years ago our school organized a student fire patrol which took sole charge of calling and patrolling all fire drills in the school. This year these boys elected Captain Norman Boehm, who took charge of the twenty required drills. The average time of evacuation was one minute and twenty seconds.

Norman as High School fire chief

tion of the substructure at NYSC in Camden, the vessel was towed to the Philadelphia Navy Yard for installation of the superstructure. On completion there, the ship went down the Delaware River and into the Atlantic Ocean for sea trials. A German submarine was lying in wait for the new battleship, and the submarine proceeded to torpedo the bow and stern from the New Jersey. The ship was towed back to NYSC for reconstruction.

Working in an essential industry, my father received gas ration coupons allowing him fuel necessary to commute between Washington and Camden. Other amenities such as the food staples mentioned above were available on the "Black Market", and he took advantage of it.

I enjoy recalling being with my father for one summer week in Camden during his employment at NYSC. He had acquired a room and board accommodation at a Mrs. Dugan's boarding house near the shipyard, and I was housed and fed there as well. During his hours of absence at work, I would explore the surrounding areas that were primarily industrial. I remember being very proud of my father on learning that as part of his work, he had been responsible for preparation of the mechanical drawings for a new invention: an automatic pipe bending machine. If any readers of this story are familiar with the extent and complicated piping that are inherent in a naval vessel or any large ship, the achievement of an automatic pipe bending device is remarkable. The number of bends and turns that must be executed is extensive. The machine developed at NYSC was capable of bending pipe up to four (4) inches in diameter, and it replaced the old-fashioned method of heating the pipe before and while bending. The shipyard obtained a patent on its pipe bender, and my father's name is on that original patent as part of the team that developed and built the machine. Yes, I was really proud of him.

THE BIG BANDS AND DANCING

My high school years were the years of the "big bands". My friends and I, that had now expanded to include boys from the town itself, became big band enthusiasts. Our group included Bert Schalk, Walt Dunlap, Cosmo Pulari, Jim Count, Jim (Basil) Upton, his brother Bill Upton and me. We gathered to listen to 78 rpm records. We held contests to see who could identify the big band playing a song not heard before. On occasion, a group of us would take a 6:00 AM Lackawanna commuter train from Washington to Hoboken where we would take the Hoboken Tube into Manhattan, New York City. With good timing between performances, sometimes in one day, we could manage to see in person as many as three big bands on the stages of theaters in the Broadway/Times Square area. I cannot recall all the bands we saw this way, but it included some notable ones such as Duke Ellington, Glen Gray, Tommy Dorsey, Gene Krupa, Jimmy Dorsey, Johnny Long, Sammy Kaye, Cab Calloway to name a few. My favorite big band was Eddy Duchin, perhaps because he was a wonderful pianist, he had a Chopin theme song, and he was featured at the piano. My friends often teased me that Eddy Duchin did not have a great band, but I was loyal to him and faithfully acquired all his

records. Together with my mother, I managed to see Eddy Duchin in Philadelphia as well as Xavier Cugat, the rumba king.

My scholastic achievements in high school certainly surpassed my athletic achievements, and it was just as well, because it prepared me for later
entrance to college. I was enrolled in the College Preparatory category and
had a straight "A" average in high school except for English that I was less
interested in than mathematics and sciences. However, my English courses
must have "sunk in". English was taught by the two Stone sisters (both
spinsters) who really confused me on grammar and the reasons for it. I
managed to struggle along with the grammar, and when it finally came to
composition, I was tragically embarrassed that one of the sisters character-
ized one of my compositions as "dull and insipid". To my credit, I took this
as a challenge, and thereafter I wrote my first successful composition entitled
"The Customer Who Lisped". It depicted a clothing store customer who tried
to explain (while lisping) to a salesperson his desire to purchase various
pieces of clothing. For this composition, I received an "A". My work in other
classes was uneventful, as I just did very well including two years of Spanish. One achievement was in Geometry. We were given a problem to solve
the total street area of a triangular intersection of three roads given a minimum of dimensional data and knowing angles. Staying up until about 3:00
AM, I managed to determine the correct area, the only one in my class who
solved the problem. In my sophomore year, I was elected to the National
Honor Society for scholastic achievements and participation in school activities. This honor was short-lived because I decided that I did not have time to
sell war saving bonds as the school principal had decided Honor Society
members must do. Explaining to my parents that school work, sports, piano
lessons, walking a new dog "Mac", etc. consumed most of my time, I did not
have extra time to sell war saving bonds. They were supportive of my position and advised the principal accordingly.

My interest in the big band craze also led me to a desire to dance. Learning to dance became available for me when the high school girls offered
lessons for five cents per hour. I took advantage of this opportunity in the
autumn during the school football season that I was not involved in. So, with
this new capability of dancing the "fox-trot" and the "jitterbug", I was able to
attend the Sunday night dances held in the hall behind Jensen's Ice Cream
Parlor. For these dances, the music was provided by Harry Ley's Starlighters,
a group of high school students, with Harry the leader of the band and
pianist. For some reason, now I can only recall three other band members,
but I know there were more. The Starlighters played big band arrangements
such as Woody Herman's "Woodchoppers Ball", Glenn Miller's "In the
Mood" and the like. These dances were very popular, however, local boys
like myself found it difficult to get dances with the local girls and this
phenomenon continued with dating. The local girls preferred the much more

physically mature young men of Italian ancestry from the surrounding areas that were the athletic heroes of the high school. This situation was changed dramatically when the Western Union Company opened an operator's training facility in Washington immediately above Pop Hixon's Ice Cream parlor. The girls were brought from nearby states for training of three months or so, and they were housed in homes of local families. As they were already high school graduates, most were older than fellows like I, however, at last we were able to get dances and dates. I even took one of the Western Union trainees to the Junior Prom. I remember her name Terry.

MY FIRST KERRY BLUE TERRIER

A new dog, a Kerry Blue Terrier came into our family when I was about fifteen. At that time, my father worked for his cousin Sid McIntee from Chicago installing industrial furnaces at plants along the East Coast. Although it meant being away from home, he always maintained "You have to go where the work is" and no longer being employable by my grandfather whose shade business had failed, and after New York Shipbuilding, he sought work elsewhere. One of his assignments took him to Caldwell, New Jersey, and there he met a breeder of Kerry Blues, a breed that he quickly became fond of. A male Kerry Blue had been returned to the breeder by a young couple going through divorce. The dog was offered to my Dad for free, so one weekend, he returned with the dog that on opening of the car door dashed out and chased our poor male cat "Whitey" up a telephone pole. After three weeks of disciplining, the dog given the Irish name of "Mac", finally accepted that he was not to harm "Whitey". But he loved to torment the cat by drinking water, making sure his jowl whiskers were very wet, and then letting the water drip on the cat. "Mac" became dearly loved by all. He was my companion, he obeyed my father the best, and he loved my mother the most. If she was at home alone and left the bathroom door open while bathing, "Mac" would invariably invade her bath by jumping into the bathtub to join her. "Mac" became famous for his performances at Mountain Lake. One of his stunts would be to leap out of an open car window, race down an embankment to the lake shore where he would leap as far out as he could into the water. A greater feat of bravery was to leap from the 20 feet diving tower into the lake. He usually began this feat by climbing up two flights of a very steep ladder, racing over the diving board and then taking his leap into space and the lake. From the height of the tower, Mac would find himself going quite deep into the water, and he would break the surface with eyes completely covered by hair. If not restrained for a rest, "Mac" would repeat the whole act again. He was tireless in his enjoyment of the water. If taken out onto the lake in a row boat, he would repeatedly jump from the boat into the water and have to be helped back into the boat. After a day at the lake when we rented a cottage, Mac would be exhausted and sleep for hours. As I mentioned above, "Mac" did become famous, and one weekend a gentleman from New York City offered my father $250 for our dog. My father's reply was "You could not buy "Mac" for a million dollars". After I departed for college in September of 1945, I was saddened by the news that "Mac" had been poisoned and died. My father suspected it was the cruel act of a neighbor, and not realizing he had been poisoned, the dog was given water that should not have been given to him. "Mac's" last act before he died was to climb the steps from the basement to let out one "woof" and awaken my mother.

Norman with his children: Erik, Kurt and Kara

If I were to offer advice to my grandchildren or any young people, this would be a good point in my story to do so. Well, as one might guess, I like to give advice, so here it is:

- Study and study hard, at the same time do not neglect studies not to your preference. Prioritize your time such that all studies are covered.

- Do not let sports take priority over studies. Learning will benefit one more.
- Learn at least one foreign language, particularly one of international use.
- Learn to play a musical instrument both for its pleasure and coordination benefit, and as I have learned, it's great for entertaining oneself particularly in one's elder years.
- Read, read, read…and watch less television hopefully to learn good English (TV is often lacking in its use of the language).

MY FRIEND ART SCHAARE

I found a wonderful friend in Washington High School. Art Schaare and his family came to Washington from Boonton, New Jersey in 1944 at the start of the school year. I first saw him sitting alone in the school auditorium while we awaited gym class to start. I introduced myself to him, welcomed him to the school and offered any assistance to help him in any way. I guess Art never forgot this gesture on my part because we became fast friends although of different personalities and characteristics. I was soft-spoken, reserved, still not physically mature and not tough in nature. On the other hand, Art was gruff, outgoing, physically mature (being more Italian than German in stature) and very tough and "gutsy". He loved sports as I did, and immediately went out for and made the varsity football team, and later the basketball and baseball teams where we were teammates. By this time, I had abandoned (or was forced to abandon) friends from our "big band" group) as they all went into various military services.

My mother and father immediately liked Art, and my Dad once said "Art Schaare will be your friend for life" and how right he was. Art came from a big family having five brothers and one sister. Often his mother would invite me to join them for dinner, and I recollect being amazed at how quickly a loaf of bread or two would disappear from the table. Art was very good at mechanical things, and somehow he managed to accumulate enough money to buy a 1936 Dodge convertible, and to put it in working order. The Dodge took us everywhere…to Mountain Lake for Saturday night dances at the casino, to Allentown, Pennsylvania where we saw more big bands, and to participate in the great end of World War II celebration parade through the town. Gasoline was the big problem in those days because it was rationed along with such commodities like butter, sugar, etc. My father, who was employed in the essential shipbuilding industry, was able to obtain gas ration coupons for his travels to Camden, New Jersey but also additional coupons from the "Black Market", and he kept Art in operation with gasoline. Art was really good-natured, and he never objected when I would ask him to transport my Kerry Blue Terrier "Mac" in addition to myself. I lost Art in July 2006,

Art and Eve Schaare, Norman and Aleksandra Boehm, High School Reunion, 2001

and I still find myself thinking of him, recalling the great times we had together, and just knowing he is gone (but never forgotten).

Approaching seventeen, my time for learning to drive became a new challenge. My father was an excellent driver, and the only one I could ever fall asleep with when he was at the wheel. On the contrary, I cannot sleep when Aleksandra or anyone else is driving. Automatic transmissions had not been developed yet, so I learned with a "stick shift" and loads of practice. Controlling the car on a hill from a dead stop, and without going backwards, and to do this repeatedly was a major emphasis I was forced to master. I also had to practice parking by backing up only. After my father believed I had mastered all his regimens, he took me on my test trip. The trip included driving from Washington to Philadelphia, Pennsylvania, from the country roads into the city traffic including into the city on Broad Street, around City Hall, and out of the city on Broad Street. I guess I did okay, because I later took my driving test after reaching seventeen years, and I did it with a completely unfamiliar Buick owned by Art Schaare's father as our car a Ford was in repair and not available.

While attending high school, I managed to find time to work and earn some money. My first job at age fifteen was in Baylor's Restaurant, a small establishment serving family type meals, as a dishwasher. For my efforts, I was paid the colossal sum of fifteen cents per hour. When I received my first pay amounting to seven dollars, I remember how proud I was to present my mother with a five dollar bill as my contribution to the family finances. My next job was as a grocery clerk in the local American Grocery Store. In those days customers were waited on by a clerk who collected and brought the customer's selections to him or her at the counter. The clerk had to be able to quickly add up the total cost of the items purchased. At sixteen years old, I was good at it, and the store manager was confident in my abilities. For this work, I cannot recall the exact hourly wage I received (probably about thirty to thirty-five cents per hour), but I do remember my first pay of fourteen dollars. Again, I proudly returned home with it and presented my mother with a ten dollar bill as my contribution to family finances. My last job before heading off to college was as a painter with Joe Steinhardt, the baseball coach. He and I were employed by the high school to paint all the class rooms in the school, and this we did over the summer of 1945. Here I earned the hourly rate of sixty-five cents per hour, and these earnings my parents encouraged me to accumulate for my entrance into college.

My high school years ended, and in September 1945, I journeyed to Grand Forks, North Dakota. Art Schaare graduated a year after I did and being his adventurous self, he joined the Army and became a paratrooper, and after basic training served with the U. S. Occupation Army in Japan.

Chapter Four

College Years and the Navy

My departure for Grand Forks, North Dakota and the University of North Dakota (UND) started from Allentown, Pennsylvania (about thirty miles from Washington) in September 1945. My parents drove me there where I boarded a Greyhound bus for a sixteen hundred mile journey. Was I nervous? Yes, I was because it was the first time I was to leave the protection and the security of my parents and our home. Was I excited? Absolutely! The segments of my journey took me from Allentown to Chicago, Illinois with a bus change. Then I was on to Minneapolis, Minnesota and another bus change and then to Fargo, North Dakota. After a final bus change in Fargo, it was on to Grand Forks. The bus journey took three days. My journey is briefly described in a story I wrote in the year 2000 entitled "A North Dakota Welcome" for my university's alumni magazine.[1] My initial impression of the people of North Dakota was a wonderful one, and my impression of them has never changed. I arrived in Grand Forks on a school day about six o'clock in the morning and found my way by taxi to the school's "Old Main" building, the first building of the school founded in the year 1833. The building was not even open yet, so I sat on the entrance steps awaiting who knows what. A short time later, a gentleman named Frank Webb (who was the Administrator) found me, took me into the building to his office and proceeded to help a young man who was in much need of help. I had no idea where I was to reside or where or when I could get some sleep, not having slept after arrival in Fargo and being awake all night. As an alumni member of the Alpha Tau Omega (ATO) fraternity, Webb suggested that I could be accommodated at the ATO house initially and later a permanent residence could be assigned at one of the school dormitories. He telephoned the fraternity house, talked to one of its members about my situation, and requested that someone be sent to escort me to the fraternity house. My first ATO acquaintance was Willy Herring who came for me and escorted me to the ATO house. He had an extra "bunk" in his own room, and here I set up temporary residence.

BECOMING AN ATO FRATERNITY MEMBER

After a few hours sleep, a shower in the communal bathroom facility of the 2nd floor (there was a 3d floor as well), I was fed in the basement dining room where I met many other ATOs who welcomed me warmly. I was their guest, and all were very gracious to me. With Willy Herring's guidance as a third year mechanical engineering student, I managed to register for my first year classes in chemical engineering, my chosen course. At that time, I did not think I could ever question my decision for chemical engineering, but later on, there were a few times when "the going got tough" that I thought perhaps I had taken on too much. After two weeks or so, I found I really liked the "camaraderie" of fraternity life, and when I was invited to become an ATO "pledge" and continue residence there, I accepted. To become a full fraternity member by initiation, it was necessary to complete a semester on trial and by establishing passing grades. With a good background from high school, I managed to pass all my first courses including "A" in Algebra and Mechanical Drawing and "C" in the others. Here I had my first introduction to "scholastic humility training", as I quickly learned that university was a lot tougher than high school and that I was no longer the smartest student in my class. My "C" grades in courses such as Strength of Materials, Inorganic Chemistry, even a Reserve Officers Training Course (ROTC) which I selected over Physical Education were not much to be proud of. However, I kept hearing that engineering was very difficult and that if I could get through the first year, it would be less difficult later. This prognosis I never found to be true…each and every year was tough. I had made the simple mistake of only concentrating my study habits on the courses I liked the best, i.e. Algebra and Mechanical Drawing, they being the courses with the most homework for some reason. My mistake of not prioritizing my time to cover all courses was not corrected in the ensuing first two years of university.

I won't go into the details of the various technical courses that followed except to emphasize that my concentration on (for me) more enjoyable courses did not improve my scholastic record. This fact really "hit home" in my second sophomore year when I found myself floundering in Organic Chemistry with an "F" average going into the final exam. I proceeded to "cram" for the exam. This included memorizing every organic reaction I had been lectured. Would you believe I wrote a perfect exam mistakenly omitting one question worth five points, and I was given an "A" on the exam that boosted my grade to another "C" for the course. If I had taken a half hour each day during the semester to memorize the reactions, I probably could have achieved a much better grade. Needless to say, I was really happy with my exam success, and surprisingly, Professor Walter Moran who taught Organic Chemistry always greeted me with a smile and respect thereafter.

Fraternity life was very enjoyable for me. I grew to respect my mentor Willy Herring who became my "big brother" in fraternity vernacular. I went to UND with limited resources, and I knew that I must find employment in order to have some spending money, my parents paying for tuition, books, room and board etc. So, I was very happy that as an ATO pledge, the fraternity found employment for me in one of the school sororities. Here, for waiting on tables and washing dishes, I was able to earn my lunch and dinner meals. This was a big saving for me, and I knew my parents appreciated it. Two other young men from other fraternities worked with me, and we took turns with washing dishes for one week and waiting tables for two weeks. Two other ATO pledges and I, Jerry Christiansen and Meredith Olsen, also found part time work at a Great Northern Railroad terminal warehouse where we "manhandled" one hundred pound sacks of potatoes loading railroad boxcars with the potato sacks. I later learned that the North Dakota seed potatoes were used in growing the very famous Idaho baking potatoes. From this endeavor, I suffered raw and sore knuckles for about three weeks until the skin on my knuckles toughened. It was very hard work, but Jerry and Meredith both farm boys were more acclimated to the rigors of farm work than I, but they too were also on limited resources. These two freshmen and engineering school friends quit UND after their first year as did many engineering aspirants. The success ratio for engineering freshmen going on to engineering sophomores was about one out of five. On this subject, Professor Gus Gustafson, who was very gruff, forthright and taught my freshman class in Strength of Materials forecasted this and is quoted: "Don't think you are too smart because only one out of five will succeed freshman engineering".

As an ATO pledge, I was introduced to a form of enforced social training. During the fall semester, the fraternity held "socials" with university sororities. The sorority and its young ladies were invited to the ATO house, refreshments were served, soft music was played, and the young men of the fraternity would talk with the young ladies and dance with them. The younger ATO pledges were encouraged (forced) to do the same thing. In other words, you were forced to walk up to a young lady, introduce yourself, engage her in conversation and to dance. It was quite a challenge especially for a person who was on the shy side and a bit introverted. I will readily admit that I owe the ATO fraternity a big thank you for this experience, as it certainly benefited me in subsequent college years and thereafter.

After successfully completing the first semester with all passing grades, I was eligible to be initiated into the ATO fraternity as an "active". The initiation consisted of "hazing", i.e. exposure to a form of physical endurance, personal embarrassment and degradation. Physical endurance included not being allowed to sleep, to be the recipient of wooden paddle smacks on one's buttocks and all kinds of labor. Personal embarrassment included being called a "scum", other uncomplimentary words, not being allowed to bathe, shave or change clothes, never being allowed to respond to any words or to talk back for fear of worse punishment. The hazing took place over a period of three days and nights after which, if successful, the scum would be raised to an active membership. While having to attend all classes, the scum had to report back to the fraternity house immediately after his classes were completed or likewise after any work activities. For example, I still had to perform my work at the sorority, grubbily dressed and dirty, such that I remained in the kitchen washing dishes and not serving meals. After daily scholastic and work responsibilities had transpired, the inductee's night activities were directed by the senior fraternity members. Going without sleep for three nights while engaged in routine activities, one tended to become somewhat "punchy" or "groggy", and depending on one's personality to be able to "take personal abuse", with resultant reactions that would differ. Some people could not control their temper and reacted accordingly threatening to quit. Others, as I did, found more and more amusement with the whole process such that I could not help but laugh at myself and others being tortured. In the end, I survived the hazing and realized that I could take such pressure. Two wonderful friends were with me through this: Clarence "Casey" Emerson and Lloyd "Duce" Dussell; the other's names of our "scum" group have escaped me. We conspired to challenge the ATO actives and managed to escape the "torture den" leaving the house while briefly unguarded. Our escape took us out into the bitter cold February night wearing only our T-shirts, undershorts, trousers and shoes as protection against the cold. Our first stop was the Delta Zeta sorority house where the young ladies gave us hot coffee. Responding to a phone call from the ATO actives as to our whereabouts, the girls did not reveal our presence, but we were certain it would be discovered eventually if we did not move on. Our next move was to board a bus on University Avenue into town (Grand Forks) where we landed in a local pub and decided to enjoy a few beers until our eventual capture. Our captors did arrive as anticipated (I do not know how many pubs they checked), and we were taken back to the ATO house. Our punishment, which we fully anticipated, included several stinging/painful wooden paddle swats on our buttocks. The whole experience of challenging the actives was a source of pride to Casey, Duce and I; no matter the punishment. Later after our initiation, we learned, from one fraternity veteran of many hazings Tom Roney, that our "scum" class was the best he had ever trained (because of our challenge).

A big Spring second semester event was the "Flickertail Follies". The Follies teamed a fraternity and a sorority into performing a "musical" presentation, something like a Broadway musical such as "My Fair Lady", Guys and Dolls" or "Cats" to be judged by local notables. My experience with the Follies took place in 1949 as ATO joined with the Delta Delta Delta sorority in a production of "April in Paris". I did not have a leading singing or dancing role, but I was in the chorus and danced with a pretty sorority girl. I really liked her, dated her for several fraternity functions and endeavored to stay in touch with her after graduation, but she was not so inclined. Our production did not win the competition, but again, it was a great experience and one to be proud of. The ATO fraternity had several very musically talented members who efforts made the production a success even if we were not the winner.

JOINING THE U. S. NAVY

In several places, I have alluded to the financial sacrifices of my mother and father throughout my early years. College was no exception, and I always tried to earn money on my own. After my freshman year, I returned to the East Coast and Wilmington, Delaware where my parents had moved after my father found employment in DuPont's Engineering Department as a mechanical draftsman. I too found work as a furniture delivery man for Miller's Furniture Company, but I cannot recall my hourly wage. I also met a very fine young man named Tom Galley, the son of parents who were our neighbors. Tom had enlisted in the U.S. Navy's V-5 naval aviation training program, and under the Navy's auspices had finished two years at the University of Delaware. For this benefit, Tom had agreed to serve three years on active Navy duty directed at becoming a naval pilot and after the active duty, to return to college to complete his education. In effect, for a three years commitment, he would have his entire college education paid for by the Navy. This opportunity intrigued me, as I knew it would remove the financial burden on my parents even though I would only be able to acquire three years of education on the Navy. So, I enlisted in the V-5 program and returned to UND for my second or sophomore year. Tom Galley went on active duty and became a naval pilot. Unfortunately, this was at the time of the Korean War, and I later learned he had been killed in Korea.

Chemical engineering was tough! I struggled through my sophomore year partly due to illness. I contacted mononucleosis and wound up in the hospital for 3 weeks and missing all the classes during the period. As a result of the illness in November of 1946 and the weakening it caused, I suffered another setback that was to reoccur in later years. In chemistry class, I accidentally had cleaning solution splash into my right eye as I was washing a beaker or test tube. I immediately rinsed out my eye with large amounts of water and thought nothing more of the event except that we should have been made to wear protective goggles. Shortly after leaving the hospital in the weakened state, I incurred an infection in my same right eye. I returned to Wilmington by train for Christmas with the badly infected and discolored eye, and my mother and father immediately took me to an eye specialist. He treated the infected eye with an antibiotic "streptomycin" that was successful in healing my eye. I learned that I had suffered from a "dendritic ulcer", however, I returned to UND not knowing that I now had a scarred cornea which caused a vision impairment and that the "dendritic ulcer" would come back to haunt me in later years. Finishing my second year, I returned to Wilmington, briefly visited my parents, and then headed to Pensacola Naval Air Station in Florida.

My naval career was not notable, however, I look at it as a wonderful learning experience that augmented my two years of R.O.T.C. (Reserve Officers Training Course) at UND. Arriving at Pensacola, I already knew how to march, the Manual of Arms and such regimens. The training called Preflight included all sorts of physical activities: conditioning and testing, swimming, basketball, soccer, gymnastics, boxing (which I'll discuss later) etc. It also included courses in navigation, weather, aircraft identification, naval law, naval history, etc. and practical training in flight control. The flight control training consisted of being a pilot, sitting in a simulated "cockpit", riding over an elliptical track with an electronically controlled model airplane suspended from an overhead boom ahead of the pilot. The model plane was controlled during takeoff from a platform (simulating an aircraft carrier deck) such that the cockpit moved over it. As the model plane achieved flight, the cockpit moved along the track and then the plane landed onto the same platform. The exercise may seem simple to accomplish, however, the overhead boom had a counterweight at the end behind the pilot. The counterweight tended to accentuate any control movement and particularly any abrupt ones causing the model plane to veer off and move erratically. For my first attempt, I managed to takeoff well and to control the model as we proceeded around the track. Coming in for the landing, I realized that my approach was too high and that I would not be able to land on the carrier deck. So, I correctly "went around", made a good landing approach and landed successfully. The Chief Petty Officer conducting the testing later told me I had scored the second highest grade of my Preflight class. Having had an extensive physical examination as part of my application for the V-5 program, I was not subjected initially to any testing when first arriving at Pensacola. When I finally was tested, my eye examination disclosed that I had a problem with depth perception (probably caused by the right eye corneal scarring) which would impede my chances for eventual flight training as I would not be allowed to wear corrective lenses. This bad news effectively ended my naval career, and I returned to Wilmington just before Christmas 1947.

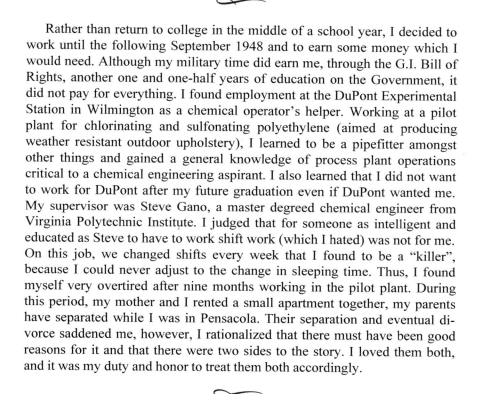

Rather than return to college in the middle of a school year, I decided to work until the following September 1948 and to earn some money which I would need. Although my military time did earn me, through the G.I. Bill of Rights, another one and one-half years of education on the Government, it did not pay for everything. I found employment at the DuPont Experimental Station in Wilmington as a chemical operator's helper. Working at a pilot plant for chlorinating and sulfonating polyethylene (aimed at producing weather resistant outdoor upholstery), I learned to be a pipefitter amongst other things and gained a general knowledge of process plant operations critical to a chemical engineering aspirant. I also learned that I did not want to work for DuPont after my future graduation even if DuPont wanted me. My supervisor was Steve Gano, a master degreed chemical engineer from Virginia Polytechnic Institute. I judged that for someone as intelligent and educated as Steve to have to work shift work (which I hated) was not for me. On this job, we changed shifts every week that I found to be a "killer", because I could never adjust to the change in sleeping time. Thus, I found myself very overtired after nine months working in the pilot plant. During this period, my mother and I rented a small apartment together, my parents have separated while I was in Pensacola. Their separation and eventual divorce saddened me, however, I rationalized that there must have been good reasons for it and that there were two sides to the story. I loved them both, and it was my duty and honor to treat them both accordingly.

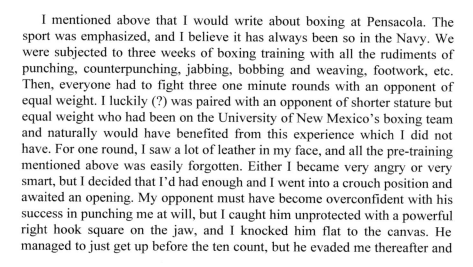

I mentioned above that I would write about boxing at Pensacola. The sport was emphasized, and I believe it has always been so in the Navy. We were subjected to three weeks of boxing training with all the rudiments of punching, counterpunching, jabbing, bobbing and weaving, footwork, etc. Then, everyone had to fight three one minute rounds with an opponent of equal weight. I luckily (?) was paired with an opponent of shorter stature but equal weight who had been on the University of New Mexico's boxing team and naturally would have benefited from this experience which I did not have. For one round, I saw a lot of leather in my face, and all the pre-training mentioned above was easily forgotten. Either I became very angry or very smart, but I decided that I'd had enough and I went into a crouch position and awaited an opening. My opponent must have become overconfident with his success in punching me at will, but I caught him unprotected with a powerful right hook square on the jaw, and I knocked him flat to the canvas. He managed to just get up before the ten count, but he evaded me thereafter and in the third round as well. I concluded that I won my only boxing match because I scored a near knockout.

BACK TO UND

So, in September of 1948, I returned to North Dakota and UND for my third year. My friends Casey and Duce and the other ATOs greeted me excitedly and warmly. Scholastically, my record improved with better health than I had experienced in my second year. I continued to participate in the University's Intramural Sports Program playing basketball and baseball on the ATO team. Baseball in North Dakota in the Spring can be a telling and chilling experience. Temperatures often dropped to just above freezing such that numb hands made it difficult to grip the ball, the gloved hand would sting with each caught ball, and the hands would vibrate painfully after hitting a ball with the bat. In those days, UND did not have a field house such that baseball could be played on the coldest days. Today it does. I like to think that if UND had a baseball team in my day, I could have made the team. As for basketball, I knew that my chemical engineering curriculum plus working part time would not allow me time to go out for the sport and I probably would not have made the team anyway. That leaves me with swimming. If UND had a swimming team in my day, I feel very confident I could have made the team. After my third year of college, I worked at a housing construction project in New Castle, Delaware loading and unloading truckloads of lumber. I was exposed to a lot of sunshine that summer, but I strengthened physically from the hard work. Back at UND, I met and became a very good friend of Durwood "Derby" Emerson, the younger brother of Casey.

Returning to UND in 1999 (49 years after my graduation) with Aleksandra as part of our western trip, I was able to meet Derby and his wife Shirley in Grand Forks as well as Casey and his wife Bernice in Bozeman, Montana. We sure had all changed, but it was evident to me that these brothers were like their mother and father who had been very gracious and hospitable to me as a student. Thanksgiving Dinner was a tradition that I enjoyed with them for four years. Here with my wife, we were enjoying North Dakota hospitality that I had told her so much about.

In the spring of 1950, I had completed my chemical engineering curriculum, but I found myself two elective credit hours short required for graduation. To correct this situation, I enrolled in Summer School taking four credit hours. My elective courses included Music Appreciation (no problem for me with a piano background) and History of the Trans-Mississippi West (a history of the Plains Indians).

The history course was taught by Professor Elwyn B. Robinson, an authority on the Plains Indian people. Professor Robinson instilled in me a strong desire to learn everything I could about these "magnificent people" (as I later learned they were described by Korczak Ziolkowski, the sculptor of the Crazy Horse mountain carving in the Black Hills of South Dakota). I read every text that Robinson recommended, not just reading only the course textbook, to learn as much as I could. I also achieved one of my few "A" grades. My interest in the Native American people has never waned. I am very proud that I was involved in the project of my wife Aleksandra and her book "America's Open Wound" (it was published in Poland under the title "Otwarta rana Ameryki" in October 2007, and three years later in the U.S. under the title "Open Wounds – A Native American Heritage"[2]). Her book reveals much about the cruelty, subjugation, injustice, mistreatment and cheating that Native Americans have been subjected to over many years (and to this day) by the Federal Government.

Through support of Aleksandra's Native American writing project, together we were able to meet and become friends of four wonderful Indians: Jim Humes (Chickasaw), Rod Trahan (Northern Cheyenne), Homer Flute (Apache) and Billy Evans Horse (Kiowa). In addition, we met and became

Rod Trahan and Norman Boehm

Norman - Pine Ridge Reservation, South Dakota, 1994

friends of Rex Alan Smith (Writer and expert on the Sioux Nation) and Larry Cunningham (Financial officer of St. Labre Indian School).

Finally in August of 1950, I graduated from UND with my Bachelor of Science in Chemical Engineering of which I am justly proud! Anyone who goes through the rigors of a college education can be proud. I never contemplated achieving an advanced degree. I had been short on finances for so many years, I only wanted to go to work and earn an income. I left Grand Forks having to sell all my textbooks for money, and I accumulated enough for a train ticket to Chicago. My father met me there having driven from Detroit where he was then employed with the Great Lakes Shipbuilding Corporation in River Rouge, Michigan, utilizing his experience gained during the war at New York Shipbuilding Corporation in Camden, New Jersey.

My father and I then drove to his cousin Margaret McIntee's summer resort on Pistaki Lake at the mouth of the Fox River in Illinois. Her resort was not a pretentious one. It consisted of wood frame cottages that she would rent out for the season. She herself lived in a large old-fashioned style wood frame house with a surrounding porch. Margaret was of Swedish-Irish parents, her mother being from the Bergman family of Swedes who immigrated to the U.S. Her father was Irish and American born. Margaret had a sister May, married to Homer Orbon (a one time Chicago professional football player) and a brother Sidney. I remained at the resort for the summer helping

Margaret with any and all chores including painting for which I received my meals and lodging (sleeping on the porch). At the end of the summer, my father collected me and we both headed to Detroit and for me to seek employment.

NOTES

1. Norman Boehm, "A North Dakota Welcome", "Alumni Review. University of North Dakota", November/December 2000, pp. 11-12
2. Aleksandra Ziolkowska-Boehm, "Open Wounds – A Native American Heritage", Nemsi Books, Pierpont, S. D. 2009; ISBN 978-0-9821427-5-2. Foreword: Radoslaw Palonka

Blenda (née Bergman), Carl Adalbert Boehm, and their son Carl Norman, August 1905

Blenda with her grandson Norman, and dog "Cop" No 1

Norman with his mother Erna and father Carl Norman

Norman and "Cop" No 2

Norman as High School fire chief

Norman Graduation

Norman in Navy, 19 years old

Ingrid Bergman and Norman, Deauville, France 1956

Norman and Ingrid Bergman, London 1980

High School Reunion, Washington, NJ 1990, Norman and Aleksandra Boehm

Norman at sculpture of Crazy Horse by Korczak Ziolkowski, Crazy Horse Memorial, South Dakota 1994

Chapter Five

My Working Years

Once again my father provided much needed support while I searched for work in the Detroit area. The year was 1950, and employment opportunities were few. Living with my father in a rooming house and eating all meals out, I was a real financial burden on him, but never did he ever complain of the burden I imposed. I searched for one month applying for employment at Pennsalt Company, Ford Motor Company, Wyandotte Chemicals Company, General Motors Company all in the Detroit area and Goodyear Tire and Rubber Company in Akron, Ohio and A. E. Staley Manufacturing Company in Decatur, Illinois. I decided that I had to look other than the Detroit area if I was going to find work. After one month elapsed, I was luckily offered employment at Wyandotte Chemicals at their pilot plant research facility in Wyandotte, Michigan, a suburb of Detroit. I accepted the only job offer received. My father and I tired of rooming house living and in a month or so, we obtained a furnished apartment in Ecourse, Michigan between Wyandotte and River Rouge. We even bought a new 1950 Ford that I later managed to destroy in an auto accident near Niles, Michigan returning from a holiday at Fox Lake, Illinois. I was exonerated for all blame in this accident, but the new Ford was never the same as the entire front end was smashed.

My employment at Wyandotte finally provided me with an income of two hundred and seventy-five dollars per month that was not impressive, but for me to be able to "pay my own way" was indeed a blessing. I was not happy with the company, my supervision or laboratory pilot plant type research work, but I stayed with it. In the meantime, I continued my search for more rewarding work and particularly more pay. I even reapplied to the Detroit motor companies. I also met another chemical engineer, a graduate of Notre Dame University, doing similar work as mine. He told me about the Arabian American Oil Company (Aramco) that had interviewed him prior to graduation. He had not accepted an employment offer because it meant having to commit to working in Saudi Arabia for at least two years after joining the company. I became very interested in Aramco and intrigued with the thought of the Middle East, and I wrote to Aramco seeking employment. The company paid for me to come to New York City for an interview in September 1952, and at the interview's end offered me a position in their Manufacturing & Oil Supply Department office at 505 Park Avenue along with a pay of three hundred and seventy-five dollars per month (more money!). I did not respond immediately, but decided I would think about their offer. Actually, I wanted to discuss the offer with my father and obtain his advice that had never failed me. After talking with him about Aramco, working in Saudi Arabia, etc., his words were "You'd be nuts not to take it". I immediately telephoned Aramco and accepted their offer joining them on October 1, 1952.

As a side note, about two weeks later, I received a telegram from Ford Motor Company offering me a job as a laboratory metals tester at the wage of four hundred and twenty-five dollars per month. It was too late! Anyway, I would not have liked the routine of tensile testing metal strips.

ARAMCO CAREER (NEW YORK OFFICE)

During my interview with Aramco in September 1952, the company advised that I would be employed in their New York office for approximately twenty months. After this period working in the Manufacturing & Oil Supply Department (M&OS), I would be transferred to the Ras Tanura Refinery to work in Research & Development.

M&OS served as a liaison between the refinery operations in Saudi Arabia and meeting the refined products required by Aramco's four owner companies: California Standard Oil and Texas Company through their off taker affiliate Caltex, and Exxon and Mobil. M&OS would receive the refined product needs of Caltex, Exxon and Mobil and combine them into a monthly operating plan for the refinery. More often than not, the needs of the off takers were divergent, i.e., one might want maximum gasoline and another maximum fuel oil which are not compatible. So, refinery plant balances were prepared that dictated how to meet the divergent requirements. In this simple example, the refinery might be directed to charge a crude oil high in naphtha content for X number of days (for other processing to convert it to gasoline) and to charge an alternative crude oil for Y days to obtain the high yield of fuel oil. Knowledge of the quality of crude oils was critical, and Aramco was blessed with an extensive family of crude oils of different qualities.

In those days, the refinery plant balances were carried out manually using a mechanical calculator (computers were not yet utilized). Extensive correlations had to be developed that would foretell the yields and quality of naphtha, kerosene, diesel oil and fuel oil from various crude oils as well as the yields from units that further refined the basic crude oil products into finished refined products. Further explanation of these activities would be at best boring. However, it was always a challenge to complete a total refinery plant balance and to find one (1) barrel had disappeared, i.e. 200,000 barrels per day of crude oil had been charged to the crude distillation units, but only 199,999 barrels per day of products could be accounted for. Where did that barrel disappear to?

Initially I took a room in the YMCA at 63rd Street and Central Park West and walked along Central Park South to Aramco's office at 59th Street and Park Avenue. Having to eat all my meals out, I soon gave thought to finding an apartment where I could eat some of my meals at home and at a much lower food cost. That was a bad enough situation, however, it soon became apparent as well that the YMCA did not offer any privacy or comfort. The toilet and shower facilities were communal, and I was extremely nervous and uneasy having no privacy. Fortunately, I met two very fine men: Bill Whildin (another chemical engineer with National Aniline Company) and Fritz Schneider (an officer of the Jockey Underwear company) each with feelings of uneasiness in the YMCA atmosphere. Fritz was actually Friedrich Wilhelm and one hundred percent German ancestry from Kenosha, Wisconsin while Bill from Lancaster, Pennsylvania did not reveal his ancestry. Years later after his death, I learned from his wife that he was part Native American. We three became good friends and decided to seek an apartment where we could reduce our food costs, have bathroom privacy and to exit the YMCA. We achieved this goal and found reasonable housing in Jackson Heights in Long Island. The location was such that we all could travel by subway to our office locations in Manhattan, however, I had the least commute time.

Before finding the Long Island apartment, I began to ice skate in Central Park at the Wollman Memorial rink. It was in walking distance from the YMCA, and here I discovered that my new friend Fritz Schneider was an accomplished ice skater, just like my father. Surprisingly, both skated with racing skates, and backwards or forwards, I could not help but admire their gracefulness. Fritz and I often went skating while Bill attended night school seeking a professional engineer's license. He later told me that he never obtained the license because he usually fell asleep in the night classes and this diminished the benefit of the classes. As I mentioned earlier, after the winter of regular skating, I finally strengthened my ankles such that I could skate without extra ankle supports.

Initially after joining Aramco, I had the pleasure of meeting Adeeb Khory, a Palestinian Arab born in Nazareth. He was the first person of Arab origin that I had ever met except for the Syrian family in my hometown of

Washington, New Jersey. They owned and operated the California Fruit Market, vendors of quality fruit, vegetables and other produce. Adeeb was a most likeable person, soft-spoken, smiling, a little on the rotund side and balding. Everyone in the office liked him. As a chemical engineering graduate of the University of Texas, married to a Texas girl, he was on a three months training assignment in M & O S before transfer to an Exxon affiliate in Caracas, Venezuela. At lunch one day, Adeeb related a very sad story about his family. Shortly after the partitioning of Palestine in 1948, Zionist thugs broke into his home and brutally removed his father and elder brother. Neither father nor brother were ever heard from or seen again by Adeeb's family. I have never forgotten this story, and looking back, it was the beginning of my compassion for the Palestinian Arab cause. Later, the noble peace prize awardees Nelson Mandela, Bishop Desmond Tutu and President Jimmy Carter were involved in that issue.

After twenty months in New York City, Aramco was ready to transfer me to Arabia and my first assignment at its Ras Tanura Refinery. My farewells to my mother and father were indeed sad ones, but I knew very surely that they were happy for me. As parents, they were supportive of the great adventure that was unfolding for me knowing that I was doing something I wanted to do. Yes, it was a great adventure about to unfold.

ARABIAN ADVENTURE–BACHELOR DAYS

Here I was, a young man of 26 years, out in the Ras Tanura Refinery in July of 1954, a new member of the Research & Development (R & D) group, and faced with a very challenging problem: how to make the quartz burning operation successful? The Refinery's catalytic polymerization unit utilized a reactor with phosphoric acid on a bed of quartz to convert olefin gases into a high octane gasoline component. Over a period of time, the reaction caused carbon to build up on the quartz bed. The carbon had to be burned off the quartz to make it reusable. To achieve this goal, Refinery Operations had built an inclined 16 inch pipe, rotated by motor-driven wheels on which the pipe rested. At the lower end of the pipe, a large gas-fired furnace burner was aimed into the pipe. As quartz was shoveled into the higher end of the pipe, it would flow down the rotating pipe to be fired by the flame from the burner. For some reason the system was not working, and the burner flame was constantly being snuffed out. Watching the operation, I observed that too much quartz was being shoveled into the higher end of the pipe by a little Saudi Arab worker. How was I to convey this observation to him? Having just matriculated from Aramco's language school in Sidon, Lebanon[1] a few weeks earlier, I called upon my vast Arabic talents achieved from the two week course. To the Saudi Arab worker, I spoke in Arabic:

"Saddigy, shugalek shugel muhim". (My friend, your job is an important one.)
"Tahut wahid shawal, oisber wahid dagiga". (Put one shovel, wait one minute.); then I repeated:
"Tahut wahid shawal, oisber wahid dagiga". (Put one shovel, wait one minute.)

The little Saudi immediately understood and began to intersperse the shovelfuls with a wait. Low and behold, the quartz burning operation started and continued to work smoothly. The little Saudi worker was all smiles and very proud that things were going well. He turned to me, still smiling and said:

"Saddigy, tkellem wajid Arabiy, al-hamdu lil-lah". (My friend, you speak much Arabic, praise be to Allah.)

Having accomplished so much with so little effort, I began to feel that perhaps my "Arabian Adventure" was starting to look promising. Up to this point, which was about a month after my arrival, everything that I had experienced had given me second thoughts. As mentioned earlier, my "Arabian Adventure" had actually begun in the Summer of 1952 while working for Wyandotte Chemicals Corporation in Wyandotte, Michigan near Detroit.

My experience of "having second thoughts" began on the flight from Beirut to Dhahran in mid-July 1954. Looking down from the window of Aramco's big DC-6b, I saw nothing but desert, mile after mile of barren, harsh sand unbroken by any green. The only feature other than the desert was the Trans-Arabian Pipeline (Tapline) which the aircraft route partly followed. Certainly, up to this point, everything had been more or less interesting, if not pleasurable including two days and nights stay in Rome (to use up vacation time being compatible with Aramco's airline schedule and management agreement) and the two weeks Arabic language and culture course at its training center in Sidon, Lebanon.

Here, coupled between six days per week of schooling, I managed to fight off bouts of dysentery (aided by the school director's sage advice to drink lots of tea or lemonade) and experienced the constant "moaning" of a returning construction engineer who was billeted in the same room as I. Arriving on a weekend, he never left his bunk bed that I observed. After not appearing in classes on Monday, the school authorities came to check on him (still "moaning") and removed him to the clinic. I later learned that the engineer had been previously discharged from the company because of alcoholism. Somehow, his record was not discovered, he was processed as any other new employee, and left Aramco's plane in Beirut with a carryon bag full of alcoholic beverages which he continued to consume in my room. Needless to say, sleeping was a lot more restful after he was removed.

All was not bad in Sidon! I enjoyed the Arabic training and was commended by one of the teachers for my excellence in pronunciation which was attributed to my ancestry. It seems that, at least in the opinion of my instructor, those of German and Dutch ancestry had it easier with pronunciation than others (Arabic being guttural as they are). It was great fun to hear Arabic pronounced by, for example, someone with a Texas accent. The opportunity to visit Beirut, experience some nightlife and to visit the Roman ruins at Baalbek in the company of other trainees was a lot of fun. One, in particular I met while processing for transfer, was Dick Winkler who happened to be from Philipsburg, New Jersey, only fifteen miles from my hometown of Washington, New Jersey. It turned out that we had played baseball against each other while in high school. On one weekend, a few of us visited the beach at Beirut, and we were enchanted by a very pretty Lebanese girl who we finally managed to engage in conversation. Much to our surprise and amazement, she responded in perfect English. She was an American of Lebanese ancestry from Cleveland, Ohio visiting relatives in Beirut and kindly engaged us in conversation. Together with this friendly girl, we sampled the wonderful Lebanese beer "Laziza".

Again I experienced "second thoughts" on arrival mid-July 1954 in Dhahran at the old open-ended Quonset hut airport terminal. Here, as many like me, I was subjected to customs clearance (including disappearance of my passport) while at the same time physically being abused by a degree of sandblasting caused by strong winds blowing through the terminal. If this was not uncomfortable enough, the sandstorm (I later learned this to be a "shamaal") was accompanied by the highest temperature I had ever experienced. It was probably at least 117-118 degrees Fahrenheit in the shade where temperatures were normally measured. After clearing customs, which included a thorough search of my luggage and deposition of considerable sand into the contents, I was assigned a taxi to transport me to Ras Tanura. I knew this was about a forty mile drive, and as the taxis were not air conditioned in those days, I anticipated much discomfort. I always related this drive to whomever I told about it as like "driving in front of a long row of steel mill blast furnaces". Having visited a steel mill on a field trip prior to university graduation, I knew the feeling. It was hot, and I perspired constantly!

My arrival in Ras Tanura and my delivery to the District Housing Office was a relief in that I finally experienced air conditioning. What a pleasure to enter a cooled room! After being logged in, receiving a room assignment and keys, linens and an advance supply of Saudi riyals to cover forthcoming expenses, I was shown to my room in the old Construction Camp employee housing. To say the least, these accommodations were far from first class. A long hallway with, as I recall, about six rooms on each side of the hall, a center section of communal bath and toilet facilities, then a mirror image of the long hallway and rooms was the design of these facilities. For sure, no aspiring architect ever expended his talents on the design of what were called "berasities". These living accommodations left a lot to be desired in that the walls were of drywall without any acoustic quality whatsoever. One could hear everything in the adjacent rooms, but thank goodness, the air conditioning worked. Well, I looked at this next "second thoughts" item as a challenge. If others could tolerate living in a "sheepshed" as they were dubbed, I could too.

After unpacking and enjoying an extended shower and shave, I felt I was ready to take on the company Dining Hall where everyone on bachelor status ate their meals. The Dining Hall was quite near my "sheepshed", however, before I reached it, I had managed to work up a full sweat once more. This experience was to be relived time and time again that Summer, i.e. be clean and dry, go outside and become soaking wet, cool off inside and hopefully with enough time dry off, then go out to start the cycle all over again. Entering the Dining Hall and ready to partake of my first meal in Ras Tanura, I ran into Joe Papso who had preceded me by a few months from the New York office and was now a veteran field employee. Enjoying my dinner with someone I knew and not completely alone was a relief, and Joe introduced me to a Saudi waiter (whose name I believe was Ibrahim). This waiter engaged all new language training graduates with the "Dining Hall" conversation which was a fixed rote exchange taught at Sidon. Other fixed exchanges included: a new Saudi acquaintance, at the "Suq" (the market), in the Shop etc. Amazingly, Ibrahim knew it perfectly, and if you did not respond correctly, you were admonished. After dinner, Joe introduced me to the Recreation Hall where employees met to relax, have a hamburger and soft drinks, go bowling, play cards (and there were some very serious card players who played some very high stake poker games) and "craps".

MEETING AN OLD ACQUAINTANCE

Here, on the other side of the world, I ran into Jim Fitzpatrick, an engineering classmate from the University of North Dakota. Jim had left to attend Notre Dame, had graduated in electrical engineering and found his way to Saudi Arabia as I had. We had been quite good friends, so this was surprising that we should meet again in Saudi Arabia of all places. Joe led me back to my "sheepshed" and promised to lead me to the R & D office the next morning for my first workday.

Entering the R & D office that was in the refinery and not the same area as the sheepsheds, Dining Hall and Recreation Hall, I was introduced to Tom Arnold, a Texan, very soft-spoken and of professorial countenance who was to be my new boss. Tom welcomed me most graciously, and talked about the work I would be engaged in, i.e. technical support for the Refinery process-ing units. Tom, having both seniority and job qualifications, was entitled to live in one of the seven unit apartments in the residential section of Ras Tanura. Sharing this apartment with another senior person "Swede" Lenerose (head of the Engineering Drafting Section), the two were the hosts of week-end bachelor parties which seemed to be a dire necessity for the engineers in R & D. There was a party every Thursday evening, but that is another story. Tom had a very dry sense of humor, loved to relate his experiences in Arabia, and he had the honor of coining one of the most famous R & D sayings. One day he decided to approach Management for an increase in pay feeling that he had been overlooked long enough. Disappearing from the office for well over an hour, he returned looking rather glum, but ready to face the anxious questions of his colleagues. His response was "In lieu of money, kind words!" A logbook of such sayings was retained in the R & D office that incidentally was the forerunner of the modern "open plan office". One room served as the space for eight engineers. Needless to say, the distraction level was very high. Tom Arnold was known to always count the number of days he faced until his next vacation, and he accompanied this ritual with his technical representation of his "happiness curve". If one can visualize a graph with "happiness on a scale of zero to one hundred" as the vertical coordinate and "number of days" as the horizontal coordinate, Tom's happi-ness curve was flat until vacation time when it immediately peaked. He finished his two year contract and returned to Texas, sorely missed by all.

My colleague Joe Papso gave me my first tour of the Refinery and its process units. In those days, the control rooms were not air conditioned, so there was no relief from the heat. My first tour left me physically exhausted, but the climax came when I sampled the drinking water from a fountain in the Crude Distillation Unit control room. The water was untreated (very salty to the taste) and certainly not palatable to Americans, however, the Saudi operators were accustomed to it. It did not bother them. Later, treated water was provided to all the Refinery units and much later air conditioning came as well. So, to work in the Refinery, I continually experienced the soaking wet outside, drying out back in the office, and soaking wet outside once again routine. The transportation from the bachelor living area to the Refin-ery was by foot, about a fifteen minute walk, and more than enough to be wet down by perspiration. Eventually, we were assigned English-built Raleigh bicycles for transportation, and although they afforded time saving in going to and from work, they only provided a minimal effect in staying dry during the hot months. Another mode of transportation was provided for work-related transport needs . . . the use of three wheeled Italian-made motor scooters called "Apes". These scooters had a small flat-bed storage built on for carrying things such as bottles and bomb samples which we used to transport to the Laboratory for analysis. Unfortunately, many users of the

Apes were prone to exceed their speed and stability limitations. There were quite a few accidents which resulted in their demise from Refinery service.

RECREATION

How about recreation? Prior to leaving the New York office, my first supervisor Bob Ryrholm imposed an edict on me that I had to take up golf if I wanted to exist in Saudi Arabia as a bachelor employee. I adhered to his edict, purchased a new set of golf clubs, and on their arrival took up the sport (without any lessons). By this time, to maintain a degree of normality, I had realized that it was very important to stay busy in one's spare time, so the challenge of golf was an integral part of my recreation. Incidentally, Bob Ryrholm eventually became a vice president of Aramco and deservedly so, as he was the most dedicated, hard working employee I met during my years with Aramco. As my first supervisor, he was much respected, as he had an easy way of critiquing one's work such that it was actually fun. If he found something wrong, he would raise and lower his eyebrows a couple of times, presume to extract a small notebook from a pocket and then pretend he was noting your mistake in the notebook for future reference. This act never failed to break me up! My venture into the challenge of golf found me usually playing with R & D colleagues Joe Papso, Jim Malina and Stan Pavilon. These three were of Czech, Greek and Lithuanian ancestries respectively. Coupled with my German/Swedish ancestry, we took on the Ras Tanura golf course as a League of Nations foursome. Stan Pavilon was a big guy standing at six feet four inches, and he could really drive the ball, however, his temper was as big as he was, and often got the best of him. On at least two occasions, he entertained us by wrapping a club around a palm tree (the only vegetation on the course except for scrub grass). He also had a very sarcastic sense of humor and managed to dub each of us with a nickname, i.e. Joe Papso was "Joe Pipstein", Jim Malina (of short stature) was "Ibn Saud-off", and I was "Norman LaBeans". With his sarcasm, he coined many other unquotable expressions, but one in particular will serve as a good example: When one of his married colleagues mentioned that he planned to take a vacation to Paris accompanied by his wife, Stan quipped "Why that's like taking a hamburger to a banquet!". We had a lot of heartaches at golf, a lot of laughs and lot of moral support for each other. None of us were great golfers, but I have to admit I was probably the worst (my game improved later after transfer to Dhahran where I utilized the driving range with a lot more practice).

Golf was not my only form of recreation. I took up bowling, and played basketball which was a disaster as we only had six players on the Ras Tanura team . . . all of us were usually exhausted at half time. But here again, I met someone from the past. It was Al Porto, a member of the Abqaiq team, who had been in the same company as I at Navy Pre-flight School in Pensacola, Florida. Surprisingly, we had even played basketball together on weekends when we were restricted to the base. He was an excellent player, and led his team in a resounding trouncing of our team. I also tested the 95 degree Fahrenheit (35 degree Celsius) summer water of the Arabian Gulf. My swimming expeditions shortly resulted in severe ear infections that the company doctor advised me were due to fungi in the warm Gulf water. This was a personal confirmation of Aramco's design criteria of 95 degrees Fahrenheit for water temperature used in its process heat exchangers, but swimming in the Gulf offered no refreshment in the summer. Later in Dhahran, I was able to swim in the Company pool and never experienced any ear problems again and thank goodness for that, because the ear infections were very painful.

Another physical impairment plagued me on this first assignment. A recurrence of an eye infection that I had suffered in college occurred. Called a "dendritic ulcer", treatment of the ulcer tended to leave a scarring of the cornea. My experience in college found the doctor utilizing the antibiotic streptomycin for treatment that was successful. Not this time! My doctor, a Dutchman (his name Dr. Mohl), showed me an article from an ophthalmology periodical which recommended the use of iodine for treatment if streptomycin was unsuccessful. I was now in the Dhahran Hospital and ready for any relief, so Dr. Mohl proceeded to paint my dendritic ulcer with iodine. He advised me that if the pain became too severe, my nurse was authorized to provide me with a pain killer. Confident of my tolerance for pain, I said I would have no need for a pain killer. One half hour later, I was climbing the wall of my hospital room with pain I could not tolerate, and I had to ask the nurse for relief. It was amazing to me that my eye doctor was so up to date that he was able to help me. Better yet, following up later with Dr. Mohl, I learned that the previous scarring that I had suffered was diminished by the iodine treatment and an improvement in my vision.

Well, recreation was not all of an athletic nature. There was social recreation as well. For the bachelor crowd, the weekend meant a party at Tom Arnold's and Swede Lenerose's apartment. These parties were, in most cases, attended by the bachelors of R & D, other engineering types, company bachelorettes, occasionally a married couple or couples. There was a lot of talk about our circumstances, what Aramco ought to be doing to better support the morale of its bachelor employees, plans for the next vacation, memories of the previous vacation, ventures into the stock market . . . and beverage consumption, lots of beverage consumption. This latter endeavor often resulted in a person departing from the party, but physically still being there lying prone on the floor oblivious to surrounding activities. One such bachelor had the reputation of doing this quite often, and after each time it happened, he would awaken, arise and spout out the words "Where the - four letter word - is everybody?" His awakening usually occurred when the party had begun to wind down. Then, on Saturday morning, he would go around to any females who had been in attendance and apologize for his language.

Christmas in Ras Tanura in 1954 could not have been too eventful, as I have no strong remembrance of the holiday. My main recollection was that my father and stepmother Marien sent me a miniature artificial Christmas tree that was decorated with a few painted wooden candles and colored glass ornaments. The little tree arrived before the holiday, and it certainly reminded me of more enjoyable times at home with friends and family. I placed the tree on the metal chest of drawers (standard Aramco issue) in my room such that it was the first object I saw when entering. Trying to recall this time is very difficult, so I suspect I spent a good portion of the time reading or working since Christmas was not celebrated by the company because it is not a Muslim holiday. New Years was another story. My old friend Jim Fitzpatrick, new friend Aramcon Dick Winkler, and I planned a visit to Bahrain Island over a three day weekend. We anticipated the joy of going elsewhere, being able to have a few beers (Bahrain was an open port) and to relax. Our venture was blessed by an invitation to visit the Bahrain Petroleum Company's (Bapco) employee camp and recreation facilities presented to us by a former Bapco employee now working for Aramco. In those days, the hotel accommodations were minimal, but we managed to survive them (floor level toilet and all), and managed to find a few places to enjoy a European brand of beer. As I recall, our first was the Danish beer Tuborg, and we all agreed that no beer ever tasted as good as that one. In the evenings, we visited the Bapco facilities and were warmly accepted by a series of Brits, Canadians, Aussies and probably New Zealanders as well, but I don't remember for sure. There was dinner, drinks galore, dancing, and no matter how hard we tried, neither Jim, Dick or I were able to buy a round of drinks. Our hosts would have none of it, and then to top things off, we were later invited to tour the homes of these gracious people for more celebrating. We had the same experience the second night of our visit. Returning to Ras Tanura, we were totally exhausted from the partying.

Keeping busy, especially on the weekends, was very important as I previously mentioned. Aramco was kind enough to provide bus transportation from Ras Tanura to Al Khobar, a few miles from Dhahran. This permitted bachelor and married employees (and their families) to shop in a real Arab community. In the summer heat, the trip was not particularly enjoyable as the buses were not air conditioned, and after completing the round trip, one was usually exhausted. But the experience of shopping for hand crafted coffee pots and beautiful gold jewelry, hand tailored clothing such as men's trousers, and all types of souvenirs were worth enduring the desert journey. Again in Al Khobar, I particularly enjoyed practicing my Arabic. After greeting a shopkeeper with the well known "As salaam aleichum" (Peace upon you) and "Kayf haalak il-youm?" (How are you today), I was always greeted with a warm "Wajid zayn al-hamdu lil-laah, sucran" (Very good praise be to God, thank you) and "Wa aleichum is-salaam" (And peace upon you). After searching for a possible item to buy, I really loved to obtain the quoted price from the shopkeeper such as fifteen Riyals. To this I would respond with "Kemstash Riyal, aiyem harb ilena? (Fifteen Riyals, are these the times of war?) This question would invariably bring a big smile from the shopkeeper. He would know I was recently from Aramco's Arabic School, new to his country, but also pleased that I took on the challenge of his language, albeit with a sense of humor as well. Whether my query ever resulted in a substantial saving in my purchase is probably doubtful, but it was always imperative to bargain with the Arab vendors as they expected it and respected you if you did so.

On my first such bus trip from Ras Tanura to Al Khobar, I became upset when unannounced the Saudi driver stopped the bus, departed with his prayer rug, and walked thirty feet or so into the desert. Orienting his prayer rug towards Mecca, he kneeled down and prayed. After this "upsetting" event that delayed our journey, I gave more thought to the driver's act of devotion. I had to respect him for his act of faith. I could only feel great admiration for him. He needed no fancy ornate church to communicate with his God. He prayed wherever he was. This experience was the beginning for me of a high respect for Arab people, their religion of Islam and their devotion. Thereafter, I was never upset when such a similar event occurred.

In trying to recall any significant achievements of my work in technical support of Refinery operations, things are a bit vague with nothing as clear in my memory as the quartz burning story mentioned above. However, I do recall that the Crude Distillation Units (CDU's) were experiencing a problem in adequate recovery of the kerosene component of crude oil. There was an inability to maximize the "kerosene cut" as it was called. Upon investigation, I managed to determine (with the cooperation of a very proficient American lead operator named Bill Gallivan) that the kerosene draw system was physically restricting the flow. As a result, we managed to have the system enlarged which solved the immediate problem. To see Bill Gallivan operate the furnace burners of the CDU's was also, for me, a feat of shear daring. Around the huge furnaces, the noise level was horrendous, and I always experienced a considerable amount of fear being near them. Not Bill Gallivan! He acted like he was in his own home living room adjusting the radio.

After nine months in Ras Tanura, I was advised that I would be transferred to Dhahran to again work for Bob Ryrholm in the Plants & Pipelines Division (P &PL). My responsibilities were to include coordination of oil production and refined product manufacturing requirements of Aramco's off-taker companies and the operations of facilities in Saudi Arabia. I viewed this new assignment with some skepticism naturally, but I looked forward to the change of work, the scenery and that I would be able to swim again in a pool. And, the opportunity of meeting new friends and acquaintances was anticipated. Two of my new acquaintances were Frank and Margaret Webb; she also working in P &PL. Both of these gracious people offered their hospitality many times, and I was able to meet their Siamese cat "Putty" who seemed to really like me. I willingly suffered through her form of roughhouse which meant enduring many claw marks. When the Webbs asked me to caretake their apartment while they vacationed, I accepted gladly as I knew I would welcome the expanse of space compared to my room in a four man portable. Also, it would afford me the chance of lots of combat with "Putty". My room accommodations now were much improved over those in Ras Tanura, but no matter how you analyze it, a room is a room. Similar to the Webbs, Bob and Anita Ryrholm were extremely gracious to me, time and time again. The oft-repeated hospitality of these friends cannot ever be forgotten, as it made life tolerable in the harsh climate and limited bachelor existence.

Recreation took on a different meaning in Dhahran where softball, at night and under the lights, was not only exciting for the players but was enjoyed by many spectators. I had the good fortune to play on the Oil Operations team that year and won the league competition. The team always had its fans based upon an edict from Oil Operations Manager Cottie Seager that anyone in his organization had better be there and root for the team. This was my first time playing a form of baseball under lights, but even more draining was the temperature and humidity. Many times the temperature reached one hundred degrees Fahrenheit with one hundred percent humidity resulting in playing almost soaking wet. But trying to play as I had once been able to, I was hampered by reduced vision from the experiences mentioned above. So, again I visited Dr. Mohl who prescribed my first pair of glasses. With these new specs, it was like a whole new world for me as I gazed into the home plate area from center field. I could see everything crystal clear and most importantly even a ball coming at me . . . I could play baseball again! One of the Oil Operations team competitors was a helicopter service team (name not recalled). They had a player from North Dakota who was a full-blooded Lakota Sioux Indian. Named "Running Bear", he assured me socially that this was his given name and to a degree appropriately so. He ran the base paths faster and more gracefully than anyone I had ever seen. He literally glided but more like a deer than a bear.

Then there was the Dhahran swimming pool that I really loved. It was always an area of activity even for those who would only lounge or stare out into space. For some employees, this act of staring was called "A Thousand Yard Stare", and I'm not sure the person staring was doing any thinking or their mind was just blank. Probably it was more likely the latter, as occasionally I found myself staring as well. The theory was that the longer you were in Arabia, the longer would be your stare.

Dhahran seemed to be more cosmopolitan than Ras Tanura, perhaps because it was larger and more populated due to Aramco's headquarters being located there. The new location afforded me the opportunity for easier trips to Al Khobar as well. The opportunity to attend the movies was the same in each district with three American or European made movies shown each week. One of my four man portable companions was Frank Bauer who never missed any movie. I would query him after every movie asking "how was it?" He never varied in his response: "Terrific!" There was another employee that I would see each and every day in the Dhahran Dining Hall. I later learned that he was a supervisor in one of the shops. This fellow would finish his breakfast and immediately light up a big cigar (smoking was permitted in those days). With eyes closed, he would puff on the cigar until it came time to leave for work. Still with eyes closed, he would arise from the table and finally open his eyes heading for the exit. After paying for his meal, he would slam his fist on the cashier's counter and then depart. If I saw this routine once, I saw it a hundred times! It never varied.

Time was marching on, and I found myself anticipating my first "local vacation". This term came about as Aramco would pay for the employee's travel as far as Beirut, Lebanon. If the employee desired to travel farther, it was at his or her expense. I laid plans for Vienna, Munich and Paris with great anticipation. For some reason, my vacation kept being pushed back due to the so-called urgency of work. In those days, there was a high turnover of employees such that certain critical positions had to remain filled . . . at least that is what I told myself was happening to me. Then finally after sixteen months in Saudi Arabia, my time came, but I must not overlook the fact that I issued my own edict this time: " I have to have vacation or else". And my words were accepted by my friend Bob Ryrholm. Why did I decide to visit Vienna, Munich and Paris? I must admit that both Vienna and Munich intrigued me, probably because of my German ancestry.

AN EXCITING INVITATION

The excitement of visiting Paris was understandable for any bachelor, but I had a particular incentive: I had been invited to visit my famous cousin actress Ingrid Bergman and her husband Roberto Rossellini, the famous Italian movie director. I had first met her earlier as a boy of twelve years or so when she performed in the play "Liliom" on the New York stage. My father drove into the city from my hometown of Washington, New Jersey to collect her and her one and one half years old daughter Pia who then spent a weekend with my family. I was not above telling all my friends that my famous Swedish cousin was visiting us. How did I become so fortunate to have such a famous relative? Her father Justice Bergman was the brother of my paternal grandmother Blenda. So, this made Ingrid and my father first cousins, and she and I first cousins once removed (this definition of the genealogy was given to me by Bob Ryrholm's wife Anita). I was treated royally by Ingrid and Rossellini: gourmet meals both French and Italian, a high-speed spin around Paris late at night in Rossellini's Ferrari, cocktails at the home of the famous painter Jean Renoir, front row table at the Lido nightclub. This was four days that I will never forget! How were Vienna and Munich? Both cities are beautiful, but at that time, a portion of Vienna was still scarred by the Russian occupation. In Munich, I did meet a wonderful "bierstube" owner named Bauer who had spent many years in Egypt and spoke fluent Arabic. In Munich, the weather was horrible . . . it rained everyday for four days, but I managed to keep my spirits up with good food, beer and wine and nightclub visits although I had hoped to be able to make at least one trip into the Bavarian Alps.

Back in Saudi Arabia after my memorable vacation, I was advised that I would be transferred to the General Office Engineering Department who needed someone with Refinery experience. I did not consider myself any kind of expert with only three years exposure to refinery operations (it was now late 1953/early 1954), however, someone smarter than I must have thought otherwise. The main function of this assignment was to act as a liaison between engineering services performed in The Hague, Netherlands, engineering in Dhahran and the customer of these services the Ras Tanura Refinery.

THE WEEKLY HIGHLIGHT LETTER

Many of the events of that time have slipped away, however, my most vivid recollection of the assignment was the preparation of "The Weekly Highlight Letter" for presentation to Engineering management. The document was due every Thursday morning (we worked five and one half days per week then), and my supervisor Walt Dayhuff was a stickler for ensuring that the items included in the Letter were worded just so. One Thursday, I was the star submitter to the Letter with four items of significance, and Walt was elated with me. However, after writing, rewriting, rewriting . . . all morning without success after four hours of attempts, I threw my last draft on Walt's desk, told him I had had it and walked out the door. If he was angered with me for my recalcitrance, he never showed it. This rebellion on my part never happened again.

Golf continued as my main form of recreation, and I took advantage of the driving range in the Dhahran compound. Practicing several days a week at the range and then playing on the weekends markedly improved my game. One notable weekend I managed to shoot the lowest score I ever attained . . .

an astounding 86. My companions on the golf course included Dave Arnett, a soft spoken Texan and Virginia Morris, a secretary but I cannot recall where she was from. Virginia was a very attractive woman, personable, good company on or off the golf course and very popular. On one weekend, Virginia, Dave and I played as a threesome on the Rolling Hills course. One hole in particular probably resulted in Dave setting a course record (if it was kept) for the shortest drive ever. He managed a low level drive about one hundred fifty yards straight out from the tee that caromed off a "jebel" growth (limestone hill) and ricocheted high in the air and back towards our tee. His drive finally landed about twenty feet behind the tee for what would be a negative drive and a certain course record. Virginia was pursued by Dave Arnett, Frank Bauer (my portable roommate) and others I am sure. She later married Jim Bevis, a supervising operator in Ras Tanura, so he must have pursued her remotely as well.

Now long vacation time was coming upon me, and I was considering where to go. Returning from Saudi Arabia to New York in June 1953, Clint Hern became my supervisor in M&OS. Clint was originally a farm boy from South Dakota and a chemical engineering graduate of the State's School of Mines. He was a great person to work for and was liked by all. One of his tales related to he and Dick Haney, both from R & D in Ras Tanura, taking a vacation in Nice, France. Somehow they managed to find the optimum golf course. It was designed such that every three holes returned the golfer to the clubhouse (and of course the bar). Clint did not brag about his golf scores while in Nice, but he and Dick raved about the course. They journeyed on to Paris, and Clint's tales intrigued me enough to decide that I had to see these places as well. Incidentally, Clint had a great wit and innovative mind. He was one of the biggest contributors to the R&D sayings. Two of his more famous originals were: "A job undone is money saved" and "Happiness can't buy money". He also made a classic remark one day in the office. Returning from a visit to his family's farm in South Dakota, he was showing all pictures of the farm and its animals. One young secretary from the Queens named Hilda, who had never been west of the Hudson River remarked: "Clint, what a beautiful cow." To this Clint dryly replied: "Hilda, it is no cow . . . it's a bull". Hilda was one very embarrassed young woman!

So, long vacation in 1956 was finally upon me, and I was "chomping at the bit" to leave Arabia and after vacation to transfer back to the New York Office and M&OS. A bachelor's life in Arabia was not an optimum one, and Aramco tried to accommodate its bachelors with the opportunity for a change and a more social life in the States. I guess they also hoped that their bachelors would meet someone special, marry and become an overseas assignment candidate once again. Well, my vacation plans were finalized and included stops in Nice, Paris, Zurich, Copenhagen, Stockholm, Oslo and London. While in Nice, I never managed to take on the golf course Clint Hern recommended, but I did enjoy the nightlife and lounging by the Mediterranean Sea during the day. On to Paris and having become somewhat acquainted with the city during my four day stay on short vacation, I managed to see more of the city and its sights, the restaurants and nightspots. In Copenhagen, I ran into Jim Morris, a construction engineer from Arabia. We met in the Merry Go Round Bar of the Atlantic Palace. This was quite an interesting place in that one had to be careful to know where he was standing. Jim unfortunately did not. Leaning against a canopy support, the Merry Go Round started up, and Jim's body went with it, while his feet stayed in place. Fortunately, he was not injured by going from a vertical position to a horizontal position. For the first time, I was able to see and hear marvelous Cuban orchestras who played wonderful Latin music with all standing band members moving side to side or taking dance steps in unison as they played.

One night in Copenhagen at a bar, I spent some time talking with a Danish gentleman who was in the lumber business. He told me of his summer home on the northern shore of the island of Jutland and the Kattegat strait between it and Sweden. It seemed his wife and son spent the summer at the vacation home, and he traveled there every weekend after work. Low and behold, I was invited for the coming weekend and I accepted. After about a 2-3 hour drive, we arrived, and I was amazed to see his summer home was a series of small log cabins, each having a distinct function and situated in a heavily forested area. One cabin was the kitchen, another the dining room, one the toilet facility, one with showers, and two or perhaps more with sleeping accommodations. I recall wonderful hospitality, good food and drinks and a swim in the coldest water I had ever experienced. Coming from Arabia with thinner blood, no matter how vigorously I swam, I could not get warm in the Kattegat. As a complete stranger, I could not forget such warm hospitality by this Danish family.

I have always believed that in all my travels, I have never seen a more beautiful city than Stockholm. When the weather is good, and it was the several days I visited Stockholm, the natural setting on the Baltic Sea made my visit memorable. I should not forget to mention that on my entire vacation up to and including Sweden, it was a pleasure to not be hot. I even had to buy a sweater! On to Oslo, and my main recollection was meeting the bartender in the hotel who had been a member of the Norwegian underground fighting the Nazis. He was extremely proud of his patriotism, told me many interesting stories of life during the German occupation of Norway, and made my time in Oslo very pleasant with the not too good weather hampering my sightseeing. I did manage to find one of the famous Norwegian ski sweaters that cost me sixteen dollars that I still have and use. Today, I cannot imagine what it would cost. The inclement weather in Norway, the first I had encountered in over a month of travels, made my arrival in London one of great anticipation.

Chapter 5

MEETING INGRID BERGMAN AGAIN

I had previously been invited to again meet my famous cousin Ingrid Berg-man who was making the movie Anastasia in London at that time. I immedi-ately telephoned her after checking into the Cumberland Hotel. She returned my call about thirty minutes later and invited me to join her, her co-star actor Yul Brynner, the director Anatole Litvak and his wife Sophie and her niece by Roberto Rossellini (Fiorella Mariani) for a long weekend in Deauville, France. Of course, I agreed, checked out of the hotel within one and one half hours after checking in (smiling at the hotel staffs' looks of amazement), was collected in a huge limousine, and taken to Ingrid's hotel. Shortly thereafter, we all left for a small airport to board a chartered plane to Deauville. The luxury hotel we stayed in was unbelievable. Each member or family of our group had his or their own bedroom and private bath, while the Bergman group had its own suite of rooms, each with private bath. I hate to think what this must have cost! The days were spent sight-seeing, having pleasant lunches in small cafes, and the evenings were taken up by casino gambling (I managed to play roulette for two hours with an initial investment of twenty dollars that eventually disappeared). So much for my being a big gambler!

From left: Roberto Rossellini, nn, nn, Ingrid Bergman and Norman Boehm, Lido, Paris, October 1955

Ingrid Bergman and Yul Brynner, Deauville, France 1956. Photo by Norman Boehm

Yul Brynner was a very dedicated gambler. One could see he loved it, and I'm not sure if he won or lost over the three days but I expect the latter as he did no bragging. One night the Bergman group went to a nightclub, and we were joined by Aly Khan and Rita Hayworth who was his wife at that time. I managed to generate enough courage to dance with Ingrid and Rita. I recall Rita complimenting me as a "smooth" dancer, and smiling when I told her that as a teenager I had a famous picture of her clad in a nightgown displayed over my desk. What memories these are for a small town boy from New Jersey. My presence in the casino required formal wear that I did not have. My problem was solved by Yul Brynner who let me wear one of the two tuxedos he had brought with him. As I recall, compensating for my height, which exceeded his by a few inches, I had to wear the trousers low on my hips but otherwise the coat fit me quite well. How could I ever forget such memories? I cannot!

Returning to the U.S.A. followed my last vacation stop in Deauville after returning to London by chartered plane. As I recall these vacation highlights, I can only again remember how grateful I was to Aramco then as I still am. My experiences working for that wonderful company and being able to benefit from so many advantages it afforded is something I will never forget. Likewise, the company allowed me to meet Arabs and other Muslim peoples from many countries, to learn something of their culture and history, and most importantly to appreciate their many fine qualities. I had the experience of a lifetime, and it continued as I did return to Saudi Arabia and stayed a lot longer than my initial two year assignment. And that is another story.

Sitting in the Manufacturing & Oil Supply (M&OS) offices at 505 Park Avenue after returning to the USA in 1956 and after my first two year overseas assignment, I could not help but reflect on those two years. Had I enjoyed the two years in Saudi Arabia or not? . . . As much as I could not wait to leave Saudi Arabia, I now found myself thinking what a wonderful opportunity I had. Even though I had two wonderful vacations for which I could thank Aramco, both being still fresh in my mind, I now found that I was reflecting on my personal and work related experiences as much or even more than the vacations. I also concluded to myself that I did want to eventually return to Saudi Arabia to benefit from the financial rewards, the opportunities for travel and the interesting work assignments and the responsibilities they afforded. However, my return would have to await completion of this latest assignment in M&OS and living and working in New York City.

I can only recall one significant achievement during this M&OS assignment. Not involved in the regular function of plant balance preparation for Aramco's offtaker companies, I was involved in refinery research activities aimed at improvement of Ras Tanra Refinery operations. Study indicated that the Asphalt Plant, limited to approximately 500 BPD production from the charging of lighter Arabian crude oils to a Crude Distillation Unit (CDU), could be significantly improved. The improvement would be attainable by charging a heavier Safaniyah crude oil (with higher asphaltenes content) to a CDU providing feed to the Asphalt Plant. Test runs subsequently proved the study theory to be correct, and the Asphalt Plant reached the production level of 2500 BPD.

AERONCA CHIEF

In 1956–1957, I became involved in a great opportunity with fellow bachelors Harry Wolf, Ray Frazier (both returnees from Arabia assignments) and Lou Kurylko. Together we were able to purchase a 1948 vintage single engine Aeronca Chief aircraft capable of seating two. Although old, the plane had to be airworthy as required by the Federal Aviation Administration under its many regulations. Our plane was minimally instrumented with only a compass, altimeter, turn and bank indicator and engine revolutions per minute. With this level of instrumentation, the Aeronca could only be flown under visual flight regulations (VFR), i.e. in daylight and good weather. The plane was kept at the Spring Valley, New York airpark near the New York State Thruway west of the Hudson River. The four bachelors now began flying lessons, something I had always aspired to even before my V-5 Naval days. Better yet, after two years in Saudi Arabia, I could afford my investment portion for the Aeronca Chief, sharing of any maintenance and tie down costs and my costs for flying lessons and aviation fuel.

The usual procedure for flying lessons entailed scheduling the flight instructor's time, driving from New York City to Spring Valley (about thirty miles) after work or on weekends and then having the lesson. The lessons after work could only best be achieved during the summer months with the benefit of Daylight Saving Time (DST). In 1957, I experienced an inability to schedule enough lessons during the first few months of aircraft ownership because of conflicts with the other owners, inclement weather and the advent of autumn weather (absence of DST). The winter season completely ended my ability to schedule flying lessons. In the meantime, two other events occurred. Our first partner Harry Wolf was transferred back to Arabia, so the three remaining partners bought out his share in the aircraft. Then, Lou Kurylko quit Aramco, so Ray Frazier and I bought out his share.

Ray Frazier had managed to acquire his private pilot's license, and together we planned a flight from Spring Valley to Montreal, Canada. As I recall, our journey took place in the autumn of 1957, and we departed in beautiful weather. Our first stop was to be Burlington, Vermont to refuel, and as it turned out a most painful experience flying without any form of toilet relief. Ray and I both had enjoyed a big breakfast with juice, milk and coffee, and the need to relieve these liquids "hit home" about 45 minutes from Burlington. On landing, after a visual okay from the airport controller, our considerable personal discomfort was happily relieved in the nick of time. The lesson learned from this experience was to always carry a capped bottle.

Another flying lesson became obvious from the flight to Montreal. Going there was routine except for the need of a "toilet facility" related above. However, our return was by no means routine, but it could have proved to be disastrous. South of Rutland, Vermont, we encountered severe cloud accumulation, and approaching the Bear Mountain, New York area, Ray was forced to reduce altitude because of the low cloud ceiling. We could only navigate by flying above the Hudson River at about five hundred feet elevation. As mentioned earlier, our vintage aircraft only had minimal instrumentation such that it was limited to flight by visual flight regulations (VFR). VFR was not possible that day! Our tracking of the Hudson River as the only alternative continued such that we even flew under bridges spanning the river (against the law) to be under the cloud coverage, rain and even temporary hail conditions (potentially damaging to a canvas covered aircraft). Finally, Ray recognized a landmark telling him that it was time to leave the river. Still flying very low, we were able to locate our airpark and to land. The culmination of this tale is that we landed with one-quarter of a gallon of fuel equivalent to about four minutes of flying time. The lesson also made us realize that

the reserve fuel tank behind the cockpit (with eight gallons fuel capacity) had
to be commissioned for future flights.

MY FRIEND BOB ACKERMAN

In October of 1957, another memorable event took place. Robert (Bob) Ackerman joined Aramco in its New York office. Bob and I immediately "hit it
off" and became great friends, and that friendship has lasted the many years
since. We seemed to have many things in common from our backgrounds,
education, ancestry, personality, etc. Both of us were from rural areas (Bob
from Pennsylvania, myself from New Jersey), both were educated in chemical engineering (Bob at the University of Pittsburgh, myself at the University
of North Dakota), Bob had German ancestry as I did, and both of us tended to
be reserved and of "low key" personality. We enjoyed each other's company
often visiting the 86th Street Brauhaus and the 54th Street Brauhaus (both now
gone) for German cuisine, beer and entertainment. As I recall, we even made
it to the famous Luchow's German restaurant, a New York landmark also
now gone. Bob was not a sports fan as I am, but once I even persuaded him to
attend a New York Yankee's baseball game at Yankee stadium (that must
have been in 1958 summertime). Politically, Bob was a registered Democrat,
and I a registered Republican, however, this never impaired the relationship
we value so highly.

Norman Boehm and Bob Ackerman, Woodlands, Pennsylvania

In the Spring of 1958, I managed to finally obtain my "private pilot's" license after moving my plane from Spring Valley, New York to Wyoming, Pennsylvania to take advantage of a much better airport facility (originally the first commercial airport for the cities of Scranton and Wilkes-Barre). Also, at this time my father and I usually traveled away from New York City to his home in Wyoming on the weekends. The main runway was wide, paved and ran parallel to the Susquehanna River that flowed through the Wyoming Valley. A characteristic of the airport was that usually very strong crosswinds from adjacent northerly mountains buffeted the main runway (blowing perpendicular to it) making landings and takeoffs tricky. I took advantage of the crosswinds to practice and gain experience in coping with them. Incidentally, the writer Ernest K. Gann devotes one chapter of his famous book "Fate is the Hunter" and relates his experiences as an early commercial pilot flying in and out of the Wyoming airport.

The Wyoming airport featured a second gravel surfaced runway (more or less perpendicular to its main runway) for easier coping with the northerly winds off the mountains. However, the strong crosswinds then became strong headwinds on the alternative runway that required "power landings" for control rather than the usual "thee point landings" at reduced airspeed. Here again, I used the typical air current features to polish my "power landings" whenever I had the opportunity. My diligence paid off because on taking my final private pilot's flight test, Russ Smith owner of the local flying school and an instructor never required me to make a "power landing". He later told me that he had often observed my frequent practices of the technique. During

From right: Norman Boehm, Bob and Margaret Ackerman, Thomas Tomczyk, Wilmington, Delaware

my flight test, he spontaneously called for me to quickly lose altitude without gaining airspeed. I was ready for this "slipping operation and quickly did a left rudder/right aileron (or was it a right rudder left aileron) that slowed the Aeronca and quickly lowered altitude. Either maneuver would achieve the goal! Russ's only comment was "Why are you leaning towards me? You won't fall out". The plane tends to move sideways when "slipping", and I was seated lower than Russ by my maneuver. I responded "I don't know".

My diligence in practicing "power landings" was the result of an earlier experience I had flying with my father from Wyoming, Pennsylvania to Spring Valley, New York. I had not yet acquired my license, but I had qualified to take cross country flights for training purposes. Our outgoing flight to Wyoming was routine except for headwinds (from the west) that reduced the normal airspeed of the Aeronca from 60 miles per hour to about 30 miles per hour and a resultant four hour trip that usually took about two hours for the one hundred twenty-three mile trip. On return, the Spring Valley airpark was experiencing strong headwinds to its main runway that was asphalt paved but only about as wide as a country road. I had not yet learned the "power landing" technique, and trying to land low speed in a three point attitude (two wheels and the tail wheel) against a headwind was virtually impossible. From these conditions, the aircraft tended to float and touchdown could not be achieved. After two attempts that I aborted, somehow I was able to touchdown but not on the runway. With poor control, I had drifted away from the runway and dragged the tail end of the plane's fuselage over runway lights. The fuselage canvas was ripped and had to be replaced. Fortunately, there was no structural damage to the fuselage. The experience although worthwhile was very embarrassing for me, but my father consoled me by stating that "if that runway was sufficiently wide as it should be, the damage would have never happened". As mentioned earlier, I learned my lesson from the experience and knew I had to acquire" power landing" capability and I did. The experience also led to my later moving the plane to a better airport.

For the next episode of my flying career, I chose a cross-country flight from Wyoming, Pennsylvania to Latrobe, Pennsylvania to be accompanied by Bob Ackerman. This flight turned out to be a most memorable one, in that it could have been disastrous. Bob never related to me that he had fears for his life, but I think that as events occurred in the flight he may have wondered why he had put his life in my hands. Well, as Ernest K. Gann in his book "Fate is the Hunter" told stores of flying episodes that he survived, I like to think that God was with us on this one.

The west-south-west flight was to be about two hundred and fifteen miles (as the crow flies) with the anticipation of headwinds all the way. The Aeronca would require the contents of the auxiliary fuel tank to be filled giving an extra eight gallons to the fifteen of the main tank. The aircraft could cruise at ninety miles per hour groundspeed with no headwind and consume about four gallons of fuel per hour in doing so. In this scenario, the trip could easily be made using only the main fuel tank. However, contemplating headwinds of perhaps thirty miles per hour, ground speed would be reduced to sixty miles per hour; the distance to be traveled in this scenario would consume approximately sixteen gallons exceeding the fuel carried in the main tank and thereby requiring fuel from the auxiliary tank. My judgment to fill the auxiliary tank was good. In preparation for the flight, I planned to utilize an air cross-country map included in my private pilot's training manual.

The map covered the exact routing for the flight, and I mistakenly concluded that it was detailed enough in providing visual flight recognition data such as lakes, railways, highways, etc. NOT SO! The map was for use in a school classroom . . . not for practical flight. Also, the majority of the flight was to be over the Allegheny Mountains that on a map look pretty much the same from the air, few distinguishing features helpful in VFR (dead reckoning). So, armed with an inadequate map and full tanks of fuel, Bob and I took off on a beautiful Summer Saturday morning. The second mistake of my preflight activities was to ensure that the "stopcock" (small valve) in the copper tubing line from the auxiliary fuel tank to the main tank was operable. This valve was critical, as it allowed fuel to be drained by gravity flow from the auxiliary tank (elevated behind the cockpit and higher than the main tank) into the main tank. Thus, I had committed a classic "boner" never to be forgotten!

The flight west-south-west was uneventful till State College, the home of Penn State University was reached. We were on course, but I calculated we were consuming more fuel than estimated above due to headwinds exceeding my assumed thirty miles per hour. And, of course, that meant longer time in the air consuming greater fuel. Sometime after this juncture, I attempted to open the "stopcock" to drain fuel from the auxiliary into the main tank. Lo and behold, I could not free the little valve. How long I struggled to open the valve I cannot recall, but it seemed like a lifetime. Advising Bob of our predicament, he did not seem to panic, but perhaps his stoic countenance was a cover up. I started to mentally review procedures in case of engine failure. During my flight exam, without any notice, Russ Smith closed the fuel throttle leaving me to resolve the circumstance. Without details, I recall the procedure as a search for a good cow pasture of more or less level terrain, once decided upon circle over the pasture to lose altitude and then land the plane. I did almost all these things, and as I was about to flare out for touchdown, Russ pushed in the throttle for full power, and I headed the Aeronca upwards. I have always believed that I could have performed such a landing on total loss of fuel and power and saved Bob and I. Well, continuing our flight to Latrobe, I finally was able to free the "stopcock", the struggle to do so always with the fear I might break the fuel line. How long was the struggle? Perhaps intermittently up to a half hour to forty-five minutes.

The next episode in my "comedy of errors" occurred when I was unable to track our flight course on my famous map. By dead reckoning, I knew we were somewhere in the vicinity of Latrobe, but the map offered me no evidence. The effect of the headwinds had caused us to drift off course. I had made an earlier southward correction to our heading when we passed State College somewhat northward from our course. This correction was a compass heading, one of the few instruments in the plane, but the trauma of the frozen "stopcock" deterred from more frequent attention to course. Bob became "the man of the hour" when he caught sight of the name of a small town "Homer City" painted in large letters on a building rooftop. This was a navigational aid used by early commercial pilots and "barnstormers" that sometimes relied on dead reckoning too. Homer City was on the map (about twenty miles from our destination), so we easily found our heading to Latrobe. Circling the Latrobe airport, I was finally given a light signal from the control tower to land (the technique used when without radio communications). My recollection is that filling up both fuel tanks took about twenty-one gallons. I guess I would judge the two gallons a marginal safety reserve, however, so much had gone wrong on the flight, I am probably not critical enough. In any event, the "infamous flight" has become a memory often thought of and amused by when Bob and I are together, but certainly a cherished memory. [2]

I am uncertain if Bob alone or the two of us together related the flight details to his mother and father, however, I suspect he or we did not. Why lead them to excess concern over our return flight? The easterly return flight was uneventful. With a thorough preflight checkout including "stopcock" operation, both fuel tanks full, and aided by the anticipated strong westerly winds behind us, we probably averaged a ground speed of one hundred and twenty miles per hour that allowed us to traverse the two hundred and fifteen miles in record time compared to our outbound journey.

Many years later in Warsaw, Poland, through my wife Aleksandra, I met Janusz Krasicki. Janusz was a career airplane pilot, holding a commercial single engine license as well as a glider pilots' license. His hours in the air were in the thousands. Relating my experience of the Wyoming, Pennsylvania flight to Latrobe, Pennsylvania, I queried him if he ever had any "close calls" as a pilot resulting from bad judgment, oversights, errors or stupidity. Janusz smiled and said "A few but I learned from them". He certainly made my day to know that I was not the only one.

What happened to the Aeronca Chief after I returned to Saudi Arabia in 1959? Earlier I had the plane repainted changing the color scheme from blue and yellow to cream and black. Perhaps a keen observer will notice this change in the photos included with this story. Before leaving for Saudi Arabia and thinking I would want to fly again after return to the U.S., I arranged with Russ Smith to have the aircraft stored. He located an empty garage that could house the fuselage minus the wings that were to be suspended from the garage ceiling. For this, I had to pay a monthly rent plus a fee for Russ' services. After about two years, I realized that my career with Aramco was not compatible with storing an airplane indefinitely and incurring the expense thereof was not practical. Again, I called upon Russ Smith to reconstruct the Aeronca and sell it. For his efforts, I agreed to pay his costs for reassembly of the aircraft and a fifteen percent commission on the sale.

RETURN TO SAUDI ARABIA

In May of 1959, I returned to Saudi Arabia to continue my career and was assigned to the Ras Tanura Refinery's Refiner's Office as the "Refiner". On a daily basis, the Refiner was responsible for determination and achievement of: all Refinery unit operating conditions required to sustain refined product production as required by Aramco's four offtaker companies, blending operations for all finished products, scheduling of product transfers from Refinery storage to Terminal storage and deliveries from Terminal storage to tankers. Also, similar responsibilities were entailed for receipt of crude oil deliveries from production facilities to Refinery crude oil charge tankage.

After a year as the Refiner, I was reassigned to the Refinery's Research & Development (R & D) group as a process engineer providing technical service to process units including: fluid hydroformer, diesel desulfurizer, refinery gas system and LPG recovery facilities. The Refinery found itself in a shortage of fuel gas for burning by process unit furnaces. The remedy proposed by me entailed utilization of a then unused crude oil transfer pipeline to deliver production gases from the Qatif field to the Refinery. My proposal was well-received by Refinery management, and I then developed the process modifications at Qatif and the Refinery to control the gas flow. For budget purposes, I estimated the cost of modifications at $60,000. Before a project could be implemented, approval of the project and its cost had to be obtained from the Oil Operations Plants & Pipelines (P&PL) staff engineer and the General Office Engineering (GOE) staff engineer, both located in Dhahran. This exercise climaxed in a "personality conflict" for me. I had no problem obtaining the approval of P&PL. However, I had a real problem with GOE and its staff engineer I'll refer to as CJW. For me, CJW came across as arrogant, superior and combative, and he challenged my cost estimate stating that one of his staff had estimated the project cost at $25,000. He emphasized his position stating that I had purposely inflated the cost like a "Hong Kong china salesman" would do. I maintained my composure (but very angry) pointing out that GOE's estimate had excluded certain needed facilities. Reluctantly, CJW finally gave his approval commenting that the urgency of the project made it politically correct to okay it. A few weeks later, CJW appeared in the R & D office, and I noticed his presence asking him to step into my office. He did so, and I asked him if he recalled the conflict we had over the Qatif gas project's approval. Of course he recalled it, and I advised him the project has closed out at $76,000. Then, still angry, I told CJW I had no problem in his challenging my work, but if he ever challenged my integrity in performing my work I would flatten his nose all over his face. Six months later, he became the head of the R & D group and my boss. The conflict certainly did not help me professionally.

A notable achievement for me as a process engineer centered on recovery of light ends for production of LPG (liquefied petroleum gas). Butanes and lighter from two crude oil distillation units were processed in two light straight run naphtha (LSRN) stabilizer distillation columns. Instrumentation for the columns was changed and operating conditions (reduction in the amount or LSRN charged the columns) resulted in an increase in raw LPG production from 60 barrels per hour (BPH) to 120 BPH. Then, a project to utilize spare debutanization capacity from another process unit was developed resulting in a further LPG production increase of 30BPH to a total of 150 BPH.

Responding to a loss from fire of Terminal LPG auto refrigeration storage, emergency operating procedures were developed to permit delivery of LPG direct from the Refinery to tankers at the Terminal. This effort was critical to Aramco as the company had just broken into the LPG production business.

After three years in process engineering, I was again to be transferred to General Office Engineering as their Staff Instrument Engineer. I received this news with some apprehension, as I certainly did not believe I had the years of experience in instrumentation to qualify me for the title or the responsibilities it inferred. To this concern, I was advised that during my forthcoming long vacation. I would be enrolled in a one week basic instrumentation course provided by the Foxboro instrument manufacturing company at their Foxboro, Massachusetts facilities. So, after vacation and the one week course, I returned to Saudi Arabia and became the Staff instrument Engineer happily for me not an extensive assignment, as Aramco acquired an engineer with the right background and experience. However, during my tenure, I was responsible for designing a "turbine metering" station for testing of the new technology meters. Crude oil transfers via pipeline from Aramco in Dhahran to Bapco on Bahrain Island were royalty measured by the standard labor intensive tank gauging technique. The use of "turbine meters" would afford savings in manpower costs if as accurate as tank gauging. The testing of the meters proved their accuracy, and eventually the meters replaced tank gauging for royalty measurement.

My next assignment kept me in General Office Engineering as one of their Facilities Planning Engineers and it was much more to my liking. The work encompassed conceptual development of refining, petrochemical and oil production projects including cost estimation and financial viability analysis required for capital budget consideration and presentation of such projects to company and owner company management. My assignment as a GOE Facilities Planning Engineer continued until 1972 when I was transferred to Exxon Research & Engineering Company (ER&E) in Florham Park, NJ as a Contracts Engineer. For this continuation of service, I must give credit where credit is due, as my old friend and supervisor Bob Ryrholm (who had risen to a vice presidency level in Aramco) was instrumental in the process.

After joining ER&E, I found myself involved in a continuing review mode of company contract types and forms, contracting procedures including contractor selection, bid documentation, bid review, bidder selection, and contract award and ER&E policies in dealing with the contractor resources. After six months, I was summoned for a performance evaluation by my supervisor who I will refer to as DS. He commented that ER&E found me as not enthusiastic and an under performer. My reaction was like a ricocheted bullet stating "For six months I've been sitting on my dead ass doing nothing but reviewing contract documents and procedures, and if I were given some actual work, my performance could then be fairly judged". DS's head snapped back in reaction, and the performance review ended.

My assignments began with performance of parallel contracting activities for three refinery computer controlled modernization projects sponsored by three European affiliates of Exxon. The multipurchase concept afforded a savings of $1 million.

Work assignments continued to come my way, and they primarily took the form of spearheading acceptance by Exxon producing affiliates of contracting procedures and contract forms generate by ER&E. Esso Exploration & Production Malaysia Inc. located in Houston were concentrated on. My services to this affiliate, and working with its Project Manager Bob Clausen and its Chief Engineer Ken Atwood, were very favorably received and I achieved an excellent rapport with them. Little did I know how this would affect and benefit my future. Incidentally, my next performance review by DS was very favorable.

NORTH CORMORANT PROJECT–LONDON

In 1976, ER&E advised me that my specific services had been requested by Bob Clausen and Ken Atwood in their new assignments as Project Manager and Chief Engineer of the Shell Exploration & Production and Esso Exploration & Production joint venture North Cormorant Project to be performed in London. Was I interested? Absolutely! So, I relocated to London and became the Senior Contracts Engineer for the project to develop 180,000 BPD of oil resources from the U.K. sector of the North Sea. My efforts on North Cormorant are briefly summarized as follows:

- Awarded $462 million in contracts while supervising four contracts engineers in all phases of the project's contracting effort, i.e. contract manpower resources, engineering design of facilities, fabrication of facilities, and offshore installation of facilities.
- Generated a unique contracting strategy for marine advisory services that broke a single contractor monopoly in North Sea development, permitted a new company to compete and saved the project $100,000.
- Improved contractor's incentive to complete work by introduction of a milestone payment concept that contributed to an overall project of $462 million, versus $600 million budgeted, and on schedule completion.
- Promoted management's acceptance of basic contract forms developed specifically for the project to replace forms normally utilized and determined as unsatisfactory for offshore oil development projects.
- Increased credibility and support for preparation of new contract forms by discovery and disclosure of profiteering by contractors performing services under traditional contract forms used by Shell Exploration & Production.
- Wherever and whenever possible, the project emphasized and utilized competitive bidding procedures for all phases of its contracting effort.

My term on the North Cormorant Project ended in 1980 before offshore installation of all facilities was completed as another Esso project was in its formative stages. The project earned its reputation as the first successful North Sea project closing under budget, completion ahead of schedule and a perfect safety record.

ODIN PROJECT – STAVANGER, NORWAY

I joined Esso Exploration & Production's Odin Project in Stavanger, Norway as its Contracts Coordinator fully responsible for contracting services to develop 23 million SCFD of gas resources from the Norwegian sector of the North Sea.

My efforts on the Odin Project are briefly summarized as follows:

- Awarded $192 million in contracts while supervising six contracts engineers in all phases of the project's contracting effort.
- Developed a unique contract form for semi-submersible drilling rig charter and drilling services.

- Surveyed fifteen European fabrication contractors to ascertain their viability/capability for fabrication of facilities.

My tenure on the Odin Project ended in 1983 with the news that Exxon was giving me early retirement. This news was shocking for me, and when I queried my supervisor as to other project opportunities, I was advised that a company-wide retrenchment was underway, and a search for other opportunities for me was unsuccessful. I have always been skeptical of this response.

BACK TO DELAWARE

Returning to the USA with relocation to Wilmington, DE, I temporarily lived with my mother in her small apartment. I also took the opportunity to be with her after so many years apart and to also more frequently visit my father and stepmother in Wyoming, PA. The inactivity eventually wore thin, and I began searching for employment. Contacting the employment agency H. L. Yoh of Philadelphia, I learned that DuPont was seeking project engineering personnel for its Experimental Station in Wilmington. H. L. Yoh arranged an interview for me, and I was given employment that began in 1984.

My responsibilities for multiple projects included design, detailed engineering, procurement and construction at the company's major chemical research facility. The projects, sometimes numbering as many as twenty running concurrently were valued up to $2.7 million, included laboratory modernization programs, installation of complex pilot plant research facilities, a state of the art nylon research pilot plant and equipment and building modifications and repairs to accommodate research programs and new research equipment. Required to carry a cellphone for contact by project sponsor scientists, I recall that I was constantly being summoned and had to keep "jumping".

Time passed until 1990 when I was contacted by a representative of Pathfinder, Inc. of Cherry Hill, NJ, a consultant in project management to the energy industry. Invited to their offices and interviewed, I was immediately offered employment as a Principal Associate, and I accepted their offer. After resigning from DuPont, I began the round trip drive from Wilmington to Cherry Hill that took about two hours. The tiring effect that the drive had on me was often magnified by Pathfinder's frequent habit of "encouraging" after hours work effort. Because of this, I always welcomed project assignments away from the home office.

My major responsibilities for Pathfinder included the following:

- In Houston, TX, preparation, negotiation and execution of contracting documents for a prominent Oil Industry Company for its developmental, environmental, drilling, and front end conceptual engineering phases for a large offshore Russian oil project on Sakhalin Island.

- Project engineering representative for a major Oil Industry Company's U. S. oil refinery during front end engineering design of its formulated gasoline project by a large Engineering/Construction Company in the contractor's Texas offices.
- Analysis, presentation and subsequent litigation support to clients in their claim activities associated with performance of contractual obligations:
- In South Carolina, for a Swiss pharmaceutical/drug manufacturer versus the engineering contractor designing a world class grass roots manufacturing complex.
- In Point Comfort, TX, for a major Japanese process plant builder versus a petro-chemical based plastics manufacturer.
- In Houston, TX, for a major Venezuelan national oil company versus a prominent a U. S. fabricator of offshore oil recovery facilities.
- In Houston, TX, contracting strategy development and preparation of basic contracting documents to be utilized by a prominent Oil Industry Company in engineering, procurement and construction of a three phase development of an Indonesian offshore natural gas resource.

My tenure with Pathfinder ended in 1998 when the company could no longer utilize my services, and I then made my decision to retire at the ripe old age of 70 years.

NOTES

1. As in September 2016 Arthur Clark, Editor of AramcoWorld, wrote: "The Aramco Orientation Center was at Sidon. Orientation lasted between two weeks and a month, depending on the nature of the new employee's job and how well he needed to communicate with Saudis. In a month, a student would have about 96 hours of language instruction, learn about 600 words and master several dozen Arabic phrases. SOURCE: *Saudi Aramco and Its People.* Tom Pledge. 1998, Saudi Arabian Oil Company (Saudi Aramco)"

2. In July 2016, Bob Ackerman shared his memoirs about Norman: "*I consider myself so very fortunate to have known Norman and to have had him as a very good friend. . . . .I met Norman when I first started to work for Aramco (Arabian American Oil Company) in their office at 505 Park Avenue, New York City, N. Y., on December 4, 1957. The last time that I saw him was when he and his wife Aleksandra visited Margaret and me at Woodlands during August, 2015. Norman passed away on May 26, 2016 at Wilmington, Del. He and Aleksandra planned to visit us in June. . . . Norman always called me WLA (World's Leading Authority). I was never able to learn why! . . . My most memorable experience shared with Norman was our trip from northeastern Pennsylvania to Woodlands in Norman's Piper Cub airplane! . . . Norman had a comment that he often said after we would drink our first round of beer- "Let's have another because you can't fly with one wing!"*

Chapter Six

In the End

My three children are: son Erik born in 1960, daughter Kara born in 1961 and second son Kurt born in 1966. I cite the events of my fatherhood here because my story has highlighted what I consider to be my most important achievements. My first achievement was the degree in chemical engineering, my second achievement was to obtain a private pilot's license, and my third achievement was to become a very proud father, grateful to God for his blessings. Whether I was a good father or not can only be determined by my performance in subsequent years, but that is another story. Perhaps the three siblings will enjoy reading a bit about their father's earlier years, but more than likely not, as interest in the father figure wanes as time passes and personal interests and life changes their priorities. Whether or not my grandchildren will be interested and read my story, I wonder. Reading seems to have been replaced by television and thumb operated digital game devices. I am hopeful that Thomas, Aleksandra's son and a journalist, will enjoy reading my story and find it interesting as she did.

The three siblings know the subsequent time of growing up in Arabia so this is a good point to end my story. I have had other important achievements and experiences as my life continued:

- Four years as the supervisory contracts engineer on Shell/Esso's North Cormorant Project stationed in London, England, it being the first successful North Sea offshore oil project to achieve completion under budget, ahead of schedule, and perfect safety record.
- Three years as the supervisory contracts engineer on Esso Norway's Odin Project stationed in Stavanger, Norway. Learning of the death of Ingrid Bergman after recently visiting her in London while on a business assignment.

Norman Boehm and Thomas Tomczyk, May 1993

- After divorce from my first wife, performing as the bachelor father of three siblings while working as a contracts engineer for Exxon Research & Engineering in Florham Park, New Jersey and subsequently after relocation to London and Stavanger.
- Given early retirement from Exxon while in Stavanger, returning to the USA, and gaining employment as a project engineer at DuPont's Experimental Station in Wilmington, Delaware and to be praised by one senior scientist as "one of the finest professional engineering managers that I have ever known".
- Experiencing the death of my father in 1983.
- Achieving employment with Pathfinder, Inc. of Cherry Hill, New Jersey as a project management engineer and providing services to major oil refining, oil producing, pharmaceutical, chemical, construction and engineering companies taking me and Aleksandra to: Houston, Dallas, Point Comfort and Sugarland in Texas; Florence, South Carolina.
- Experiencing the death of my mother in 1992 while on assignment for Pathfinder in Houston, Texas.
- Experiencing life in Poland in 2006/2007 while Aleksandra fulfilled a 13 month Fulbright research assignment.

- Being honored and justifiably proud to learn that Aleksandra's son Thomas considered me as his father along with calling me Dad.
- Continuing to spend the remainder of my life with my beloved wife Aleksandra, enjoying life together as we always have, being blessed and thankful that the Lord brought us together and relishing our love for one another. My personal life and experiences during the foregoing, including meeting my wife Aleksandra in 1989, our marriage of 26 years, our extensive travel together . . . could they be the basis for another story?

Norman Boehm and Thomas Tomczyk, Woodlands, Pennsylvania 2003

As a conclusion to all the foregoing, I wonder if passing on a short prayer I have utilized over the years might be worthwhile passing on to any readers. The prayer has "stood me in good stead", but will they be receptive to it? Why not try? Here it is:

> "Lord, help me to control my tongue
> Lord, help me to control my temper
> Lord, help me not to be vengeful."

Now, when I am retired I like the rhythm of my days with beloved Aleksandra. We have tea with lemon and honey in the early morning.

It is a good day when I am able to play my piano . . . I buy new music and am happy to learn more melodies, like "Begin the Beguine", "Adios", "Granada", "My Shawl", and many others.

Weather permitting, we frequently bask in the privacy of our rear garden and enjoy a good cup of coffee . . . or for me my favorite beer Pilsner Urquell.

Our times of pleasure include love for and interaction with the felines that are with us . . . earlier Claude and Suzy and now Rudi and Sophie.

We are able to enjoy a good movie in the evening (minus any commercials) with HBO and Netflix (thanks to Thomas).

Norman Boehm 2016

Norman playing piano at home in Wilmington, Delaware

Norman, Aleksandra and Thomas, Wilmington, Delaware

Christmas in Wilmington, Delaware, Norman and Aleksandra

Annex 1: A Flood of Memories

On entering the Riverside area of Grand Forks, my wife Aleksandra and I were overcome by the stillness and emptiness. All that was left of the once beautiful residential neighborhood were the streets, sidewalks, trees and shrubs...the houses were all gone. Had the birds left as well? The stillness made us wonder if the Flood of 1997 had forced them to leave too. How could the Red River have been so cruel as to ruin the Riverside area of Grand Forks? Then I began to recall how destructive it had been in the Spring of 1946, my first year at the University of North Dakota. As a freshman, a new member of Alpha Tau Omega fraternity and a first time witness to the power of a flooding river, I gained practical experience with the Red River which was overflowing its banks. The winter of 1945-1946 had been one of severe cold (for an Easterner like me) along with heavy snow accumulation. Our fraternity volunteered to aid in "sandbagging" the beautiful new ranch style home of our brother Bob Absy which was being threatened by the river. We labored for two days and nights building a sandbag wall around the home. Now, visiting Riverside was the first part of a tour by my dear friends Derby and Shirley Emerson of Grand Forks who had lost their home to the Red River in the 1997 flood. This was the beginning of my "flood of memories".

RETURN WITHOUT APPREHENSION

Approaching Grand Forks with Aleksandra on 20 September 1999, I did not feel the degree of apprehension that I did 49 years earlier when I arrived to enter UND. This time I knew I would be greeted by Derby and Shirley Emerson. We had been in contact for the entire 49 year period, even though I had never been able to return to visit my alma mater. Looking back, it seemed I had been neglectful, even though there was always something else to do or that my nearly 23 years of working overseas prevented my return. Well, here I was about to remedy my neglect. I had a feeling of real pride that I was about to show off my university to my bride. After checking into the AmericInn, I telephoned the Emersons who were anticipating our arrival. They were at the front entrance of the hotel within 20 minutes, and as we embraced, there were words to the effect of "how the years had taken their toll". But for me, it was the beginning of one of many memories, as I inhaled their warmth as of years ago and viewed their faces with the same beautiful smiles. From them, I learned that Derby's brother Casey and wife Bernice (also my dear friends) in Bozeman, Montana were expecting to see us. So that evening, Casey telephoned, and we arranged our subsequent schedule to visit them after our stay in Grand Forks. Through the graciousness of Derby and Shirley, Aleksandra and I toured the beautiful campus of UND which was basically as I remembered it but expanded tremendously.

PROFESSOR BEN GUSTAFSON

Gone were some of the buildings I knew such as the engineering building. Here other engineering aspirants and I were greeted in Professor Gustafson's Strength of Materials class in the Fall of 1945. His exact words I cannot recall, but they clearly implied that come the beginning of the next year's Fall semester 1946, the aspiring engineers' ranks would be purged by about 75 percent. He was correct, and the engineering student ranks were ravaged, with many entering other fields of study. Professor Gustafson was a gruff, old-fashioned and strict teacher. Everyone tended to fear him, and everyone respected him. He loved to tell the story of his Analytical Chemistry course taught to a group of New Yorkers in the Army Special Training Program during the war. Being typical young New Yorkers with smart mouths and wise guy attitudes, they irritated the Professor and acted disrespectfully towards him. Little did they know they would incur the professor's form of "humility training" because of their attitude. The professor decided to submit them to the ultimate challenge in Analytical Chemistry. For their "unknown", which was to be analyzed to determine the chemical elements it contained, Professor Gustafson gave them distilled water plus an indicator. Every analytical procedure they submitted the "unknown" to would result in the "unknown" changing color without ever defining a chemical element. Chuckling to himself, he would relate how humble the New Yorkers became as the semester elapsed without their solving the "unknown's" contents and the potential for course failure stared them in the face.

MILITARY EXPOSURE

The old Armory was still there, and here I was first exposed to military training in ROTC courses. With the many returning veterans on the UND campus, who had real military experiences, this seemed like a token effort on my part, but I did believe it was beneficial and well worth the effort. I'm sure my posture was improved. Learning a few basic military procedures such as marching, the manual of arms etc. benefited me when I did my time in the Navy. Here to I enjoyed the many Sioux basketball games including some of those my friend Derby (who was a fine player) participated in.

FALL FOOTBALL

The old football stadium was still there, but I learned that 2000 would be its last year of service and that it was to be replaced with a new modern stadium then under construction. How many times did I watch the Sioux football team face their opponents in snowstorms even in September? And how often did I feel the thrill of UND's "Fight On Sioux" to Indian drum rhythm? Quite a few!

MY FIRST WINTER

Our tour of the campus included the English Coulee. My main recollection was how enjoyable it was in the Springtime (after the long harsh Winter), to participate in the study of Surveying on the Coulee's banks and to be out of the classroom. Speaking of the long harsh winter, my first winter of 1945-1946 was the coldest I had ever experienced. Temperatures reached -36 degrees F! In those days, no one talked about the wind chill factor as they do today on TV, but I would guess it was -50 degrees F or even lower. I never experienced such cold in subsequent years at UND, but perhaps I grew accustomed to it. At the same time, I had never seen so much snow. The drifts reached above the second floors of fraternity and sorority houses on University Avenue. One evening, on my return from waiting tables at the Delta Delta Delta sorority house (my father could not believe I was so privileged), I could only find my way back to the Alpha Tau Omega fraternity house by the street lights barely visible through the blinding snow. Incidentally, for the good fortune of waiting tables at the Tridelta house, I thank the ATO fraternity.

HOCKEY ON NATURAL ICE

Being a spectator of hockey in a natural ice arena can be a numbing experience. Many times, it seemed as though it was colder inside the old Quonset hut arena than outside. However, no matter how cold, it was always a thrill to watch the Sioux hockey team perform. With such quality players as Jimmy Medved, John Noah, Joe Silovich and others, the Sioux took on the big university teams such as Minnesota, Michigan, Colorado and, more often than not, beat them. Maybe the bone-chilling cold had something do with it, but I believe the Sioux, in those years, made the NCAA contestants realize that UND was a force that would have to be reckoned with. Haven't subsequent years supported this contention?

BROTHER PAUL

One bitter cold night, returning home after witnessing the Sioux hockey team beat the Golden Gophers of Minnesota, my friends and I came upon a body on all fours crawling on the frozen snow-covered ground along Columbia Avenue. It was headed from the hockey arena towards University Avenue. On close scrutiny, we found it was Paul Bjugstad, an ATO fraternity brother. Paul had over "antifreezed" himself with alcohol apparently to help endure the cold. Having done so perhaps throughout the game, he realized his legs would not carry him, so he did the next best thing…he crawled on hands and knees. Fortunately, we found him soon enough because he had a long way to go. Paul was of short stature, a farm boy of Norwegian ancestry, who having only used Norwegian at home with his parents, spoke English with an accent. He was the most beloved of our fraternity brothers. Everyone liked Paul, and one of his most recognized achievements was coining the famous expression: "Boozers are loosers" (spoken with a Norwegian accent of course). If Paul reads this, I hope he will understand that I am only trying to portray the humor of the situation, and I, like all the other ATOs at that time, thought him as the greatest.

PROFESSOR ELWYN ROBINSON

Having completed all the technical course requirements for a B.S. in Chemical Engineering at the end of the Spring semester in 1950, I found I was short two credit hours to graduate. So, I enrolled in Summer School and took on the burden of two electives (four credit hours): Music Appreciation and History of the Trans-Mississippi West. The latter course, taught by Professor Elwyn B. Robinson, was a history of the Plains Indians. Never had I experienced such enthusiasm by a teacher who was able to convey that enthusiasm to his pupils (at least this one). Professor Robinson generated within me a life-long interest and concern for Native Americans, their culture, their history, and their woeful mistreatment and neglect by the U.S. Government. He started it, and now more than 50 years later, I am happy to complement my interest by supporting three Indian schools, one near the Crow Creek Reservation, one on the Pine Ridge Reservation (both in South Dakota) and one on the Northern Cheyenne Reservation in Montana along with other programs such as Billy Mills' "Running Strong For American Indian Youth", the Native American Heritage Association and others. In addition, I enthusiastically support my wife's current project writing about the present day status of the Native Americans. Engineering at UND was tough, and for an engineering student to accept his professor's challenge to read all extra-curricular references, I realized was a testimonial to Professor Robinson's inspirational teaching ability. Incidentally, I did not make many A's in my four years in engineering, but I did proudly make one in his course.

TOO MANY GERMANS

Awarded the Bronze Star for valor, our fraternity brother narrated the story of his bravery as if it were a "comedy of errors". Coming upon an isolated farmhouse (I believe it was in France), he and his companion forward scout approached it thinking there might be a few isolated German soldiers remaining. Calling out in broken German "Kommen zi aus", a German voice responded that he was ready to surrender. He appeared in the farmhouse doorway and readily surrendered himself and weapons to our heroes. Then, to the amazement of our heroes, a second German made his way out, then a third, then a fourth, a fifth and on and on. As the number of Germans continued to exit the farmhouse, our heroes became overwhelmed, more scared, more nervous and even forgetting military procedure to remove the weapons from their captives. When it was all over, Herman Bergeth of Grand Forks and his comrade had captured 66 Germans who gave them no opposition. He was the first to say that lucky for him, the tide had turned and the Germans had enough of war, hunger and its misery. Never could I tell this tale as Herman did, as he would have his fraternity brothers hysterical with laughter, and not only that, he was called upon again and again to relate the story. If Herman reads this, I hope he will forgive me for taking the liberty of briefly telling his story. We all knew he was a real hero, deserving of the honor bestowed upon him, and best of all a wonderful story teller.

BIG BAND AL

A talented musician who played the trumpet, composed and arranged music and best of all was the leader of his own dance band, Al Gillespie brought music, music, music to his ATO fraternity brothers and their friends and companions. Never reluctant to date myself by stating my love for big band music, I found myself under the same roof as a first class band leader. I had the opportunity to hear his band when they played nearby or rehearsed, and always thought that perhaps North Dakota might produce another Lawrence Welk. Being soft-spoken and gentle of nature, Al seemed to personify the nice-guy reputation of a big band leader like Glenn Miller and obviously Lawrence Welk who maintained his image years after the demise of the big bands. Who knows what might have happened had Al pursued that career, but I hope he enjoyed success in whatever he chose. He was a good baseball player too!

THE MISSING SOCKS

Slender, quiet, of dry-wit, and an Air Force veteran, Bob Dupont must have had many hair raising experiences as, I believe, a B-17 pilot in the South Pacific. Hurtling down the runway, endeavoring to gain ground speed and to create lift, Bob related how he had to extend his full physical strength (including propping his feet against the control panel for leverage) to pull back on the yoke. For some unknown reason, the faster the aircraft's ground speed, the effect of lift was diminished (Bob called it negative lift). Every mission had to be anticipated with fear but takeoff must have made it a nightmare. Bob and I were roommates in the ATO house, and I began to notice a strange phenomenon. My socks started to disappear! For awhile, I thought it was my own absentmindedness, but then when newer pairs began to disappear, I started to investigate. Several pairs were found in Bob's dirty laundry disposal, some well worn to the extent that toes and even heels were missing. On a very limited budget throughout my university years, I could not tolerate a negative cash flow in socks, so I challenged Bob. With chagrin, he admitted to being the culprit (what else with the evidence on hand) and offered to pay for the socks used and/or destroyed beyond repair. I rejected his offer, and our agreement was that he was to keep hands off my socks thereafter. What I could never understand was how he could wear socks with no heels or toes. But then, I had never experienced what Bob had in the South Pacific.

DUSSELL AND DUSSELDORF

An extroverted, personable and very popular fraternity brother named Lloyd ("Duce") Dussell was part of my wonderful UND memories. Duce was an Air Force veteran who had piloted, I believe, a B-24 bomber in the European theater. He had the distinction of being part of the leveling of, of all places, Dusseldorf. I had the opportunity of visiting that rebuilt city in the mid 60's, and while walking, I recall encountering a severely scarred German veteran who carried himself very erectly like an officer. He was without one eye, one arm and one leg. Recognizing me as an American, he gave me a look of absolute hatred as if I had been responsible for bombing his city. Duce and I were both chemical engineering students, and he spent one Summer with me in the East working for Hercules while I worked for DuPont both trying to gain some practical experience in our chosen professions. As I said, he was an extrovert and while attending the 80th birthday celebration of my maternal grandfather, he managed to convince many of the attendees he was a full blooded Sioux Indian (no longer on the warpath). Many years later, while working in London on a joint Shell/Esso North Sea oil development project, our paths crossed again as Duce was there as well working for Bechtel. I hope our paths will again cross!

THANKSGIVING

What was it like to stuff ones self on homemade food for four days every Thanksgiving at UND? It was wonderful! Being from the East Coast, the four day holiday was inadequate for a trip home. Instead, I remained on the campus but found that I always would be invited for a Thanksgiving dinner. If not on the holiday Thursday itself, my kind hosts would adjust their schedules so that I would be invited for turkey and all the trimmings on one of the four days. Eat I did, and it was wonderful homemade cooking. The families of Derby and Casey Emerson, Lloyd Dussell, Professor Staley (the head of the Mathematics Department) and others leave a memory that I will never forget.

CHORUS BOY

Participating in the "Flickertail Follies" was an experience that I did not volunteer for. My shyness, especially in the presence of girls, was enough of a burden for me to overcome in my university years. But then, by directive of ATO officers, one had to also perform in the "Follies" which meant dancing on the stage, with a girl (from our sorority partner) before a live audience to boot. Despite all of this pressure, I managed to dance on the stage, with

Shirley Swedeen, a pretty girl from the Delta Delta Delta Sorority, before a live audience for two performances no less. In later years, whenever I saw a musical on stage, such as "My Fair Lady", "Fiddler On The Roof", "Kismet", "Chorus Line" to name a few, I always recalled my "chorus boy" days at UND recognizing that I was not the type (thank goodness).

"HAZING"

After three days of "hazing", total exhaustion and then formal initiation into the fraternity, our inductors' expletives were: "It never happened before", "Unbelievable", "The most spirited group of 'scums' ever encountered". These words of praise from old time fraternity pledge masters such as Tom Roney made us (a band of renegade 'scums' including Casey Emerson, Duce Dussell, myself and others not recalled) proud we had done the unexpected. How did we warrant such praise from our well-experienced inductors? A few of us (four or five as I recall) rebelled and escaped from the fraternity house. Our escape route took us through two sorority houses, the bus downtown to Grand Forks and finally into a bar for some liquid sustenance (beer). Contemplating our escape, we knew eventual capture would result in an intensification of "hazing". But nevertheless, being tired from lack of sleep and the pressures, escape seemed a logical thing to do so we did and in the dead of winter lacking appropriate clothing. Our inductors finally captured us downtown in a bar, escorted us back to 3000 University and the "hazing" intensified, i.e. the wooden paddles around the house were wielded more frequently. But, the satisfaction of challenging the system, and having lots of fun and laughs doing it, more than outweighed the consequences.

SPRING TRAINING

Playing baseball in the Spring at UND brought another level to the sport. There was no field house for protection from the elements. Baseball was not a varsity sport then, so intramural competition permitted only the hardiest of souls to play the game. Originally from New Jersey and an area of rabid interest in baseball, I grew up keenly involved in playing. In the Spring, my friends and I could not start our "choose up sides" games soon enough. Later, in high school, and a member of a New Jersey state championship team (1945), we began practice early. In the North Dakota Spring, we nearly froze to death or thought we would as practice was held in inclement weather. Hitting the ball could hurt, catching the ball could hurt, and throwing the ball with numb hands was difficult...all for the love of the sport. Temperatures hovered around freezing, there were snow flurries, and the elements did little to improve the quality of the games. I often wondered later as I recalled baseball at UND, how did North Dakota's most famous player, the immortal Roger Maris hone his skills with such uncooperative weather. There were some really good players in the intramurals. I remember Joe Silovich (the football and hockey great)...he was awesome and nerve shattering on the mound. With the fastest velocity pitch I had ever encountered, coupled with erratic control, Joe was scary to face.

MAKING ENDS MEET

Going to college presented some financial challenges to your humble writer. I was always trying to earn some extra cash to supplement very limited funds. When I embarked on my college career, it was made clear by my father that I had to earn my own spending money. There would be no money available for the fun part of school. So, I looked for opportunities to make some. In the fall of 1945, Jerry Christensen, Marion Hansen (from my fraternity) and I obtained employment as "potato baggers" at a local warehouse. For six weeks, whenever we had a few hours free, we would manhandle 100 pound bags of potatoes readying them for rail shipment. I can't remember our wage, but I can remember raw bloodied knuckles for about two weeks until my hands toughened up. After making one of my few "A's" in Mechanical Drawing, Professor Heinz offered me a semester assignment correcting freshman class drawings. His first admonishment to me was that the initial set of drawings to be corrected was not to average over a grade of 50. He was not too happy but accepted my average grading of 49.75 for that set. Waiting on tables and washing dishes was part of my four year career at UND and thankfully so. I never starved, and I enjoyed some wonderful cooking. This career included one semester at the ATO house, one at the Delta Zeta sorority house, and several semesters at the Delta Delta Delta sorority house. My social graces and ability to be at ease socially were enhanced, and it was really an experience to be in the presence of so many pretty girls!

Could I go on? Do I have other memories? Oh yes, but can I continue to relate them? Probably not, but just so I do not forget them, I recall:

- My friend and fraternity brother Bill Kelly, who achieved his chosen career as a medical doctor, meeting in a Mexico City restaurant in 1959 when he hollered "Hey Norm, what are you doing here?" Bill was a good baseball player too!
- A friend and fellow engineering student I tried to recruit into ATO named Jim Fitzpatrick (who after two years at UND transferred to Notre Dame), meeting in Ras Tanura, Saudi Arabia in 1954 when I entered Aramco's construction dining hall.

- Being one of three UND graduates working for Aramco in Saudi Arabia: Mel Orseth an electrical engineer, Tom Barger, a geologist who became Aramco's top officer and yours truly as a chemical engineer.
- Recalling the ultimate one story story teller Nick (whose surname has escaped me and of Greek ancestry) who, if he told it once, told the story a hundred times, about the stuttering outdoor toilet salesman.

Annex 2: About Aramco

"Aramco", or the Arabian American Oil Company, became an integral part of my life and now a cherished memory beginning in 1952. As a recent chemical engineering graduate, I learned of Aramco from a colleague while working in the chemicals industry. My interest was challenged to the extent that I applied for work to their New York office on Park Avenue. In October 1952, I began a career with them having accepted a "condition of employment" that, in the near future, I would be willing to take an assignment in Saudi Arabia. Twenty-one months later (June 1954), I was on my way to Saudi Arabia with a two week stopover in Lebanon to attend Aramco's Language Training Center in Sidon.

From the very first days with Aramco, their supervisory personnel stressed the importance of a proper attitude in meeting with, working with and relating to Saudi Arabs, their language and their culture. This exposure to supervisors who had lived and worked in Saudi Arabia and the subsequent language and cultural indoctrination received in Sidon provided me with a strong foundation that never failed me in my nearly 16 years in Saudi Arabia. I treated every Saudi regardless of position with respect, and never did I experience any ill-feelings from them. I only experienced their mutual respect for me. Here in New York, I met my first Arab colleague…a Palestinian Arab from Nazareth and a graduate chemical engineer. Thus, from him, I first learned how warm and friendly an Arab could be!

Prior to departure from New York to Saudi Arabia, a U.S. passport had to be obtained from the State Department. During this operation, Aramco obtained a verification that their potential transferee was not Jewish in order to comply with the Saudi Government's restriction on only allowing Christian or Muslims into their country.

The indoctrination period in Sidon consisted of language training in the morning and history and culture in the afternoon. We learned that probably half or more of the people (then estimated at 5 – 6 million) lived in oases and tilled the soil. The others were Bedouins who roamed the vast desert with their flocks and herds or those who went to sea, worked in the oil industry, were employed in the government, the professions, the crafts and commerce. We learned that all Saudi Arabs, regardless of their racial origins have at least two characteristics in common: they speak Arabic and they are Muslims. They do not all speak the same dialect of Arabic, and they do not all belong to the same sect of Islam.

According to Arab tradition, we learned that the Bedouins of the desert are regarded commonly as the prime source of a pure stock whose bloodline is traceable back through the ages to their ancestor Abraham (Ibrahim) and his first son Ishmael (while the Hebrews descended from his second son, Isaac). According to Muslims, elements of their religion were revealed through a long line of Prophets including: Abraham (Ibrahim), Moses (Musa) and Jesus ('Isa). The full and final revelation was given to Muhammad and later was embodied in written form in the Koran, the chief source for Islamic doctrines and practices.

The summer heat experienced in Sidon was only a minor prelude to that we were warned would be encountered in Saudi Arabia. Summer temperatures we were told would frequently reach 120 degrees Fahrenheit (49 degrees Celsius) "in the shade" and this would be coupled with high humidity along the Persian Gulf. I later learned that this forecast was indeed true as I toured the Ras Tanura Refinery in July in my first process engineering assignment. It was a matter of starting out dry in air conditioned living quarters, becoming soaking wet from perspiration once outdoors, and then drying out indoors. This cycle was constantly repeated that summer which is longer than in more temperate climates. The spring and fall are pleasant with cool nights and sunny, balmy days. In December through February, temperatures sometimes drop below freezing.

Average rainfall in Saudi Arabia's Eastern Province is about 3 inches (7.6 centimeters) per year with a historical range of 1 – 7 inches). Because rainfall is so little, most of Saudi Arabia is desert. Parts of the country such as the Rub' al-Khali (Empty Quarter) have been known to be without rain for 10 years. Rainfall over most of the Arabian Peninsula is not sufficient to support much vegetation, however, in many areas water collects in underground strata and is utilized by wells.

As part of the cultural indoctrination, familiarization with local customs was emphasized, and great importance was placed upon being considerate of the Saudis and having a respect for their feelings, customs and beliefs. What were some of the examples of how to deal with Saudis routinely: Greet him formerly of course, ask how his health is, but do not ask how his wife is! Ask how his son is, but do not ask how his daughter is. Never become angry at a Saudi, curse him or strike him. Treat him with dignity and respect and you will be treated the same. The first and foremost common gesture of hospitality among all Arabs, whether entertaining each other or outside visitors, is the serving of coffee. The Saudis embellish this predominant social drink by the use of cardamom added to the roasted and crushed coffee beans. Most Westerners familiar with the famous Turkish coffee may come to realize that originally the coffee process was Arabic but by bringing it to Europe, the Turks managed to take the credit. I cannot remember any instance when, upon entering one of the refinery control rooms, I was not offered "ghawah" (coffee) by one of the Saudi operators. And that is characteristic of Arab hospitality.

Living and working in Saudi Arabia meant life within a fenced enclosure like on a military base. There were three main company districts in those days: Dhahran (the headquarters), Ras Tanura (the refinery and offshore terminal) and Abqaiq (the oil gathering center). Each community provided family housing: single family California style homes, single family apartments and bachelor quarters (single rooms in 4 man portable buildings or in barracks style buildings). Family housing was assigned on a point system which rated the employees on job category and service time. Many married employees suffered through extended periods away from their families awaiting the accumulation of enough points to earn an accommodation. Over the years, this hardship was diminished as more and more family housing was constructed.

There was exposure and contact with Saudis constantly. They exuded a warmth and pleasant manner usually with a smile. The clerk in the company commissary (where most of the food shopping was done), the local fisherman who brought fresh Persian Gulf shrimp (cleaned) for sale, the waiter in the company dining hall (provided for bachelor employees), or the merchant in Al Khobar (an Arab community near Dhahran) all had this nice way about them. And they had a sense of humor too. I always managed to obtain a big smile when bartering the sales price on an item. I did this by asking the merchant: "Are these the times of war?" The trips to the "suq" (market place) in Al Khobar were always a big event afforded by company bus or taxi (un-air conditioned in those days).

With the harsh climate, travel on foot or by bicycle was debilitating, and I quickly learned the importance of salt intake as recommended by Aramco's Medical Department. The good advice from my time in Sidon to combat diarrhea with intake of lemonade or hot tea also saved me. The importance of staying active beyond working hours, i.e. to avoid being bored was most important. The company provided many recreational facilities such as movies (three per week), bowling alleys, tennis courts, basketball courts, baseball/softball diamonds, swimming pools, golf courses, billiards, snack bars,

Hobby Farms for stabling and riding of horses, boat marinas, a veterinary clinic etc. Various Aramco groups organized themselves to utilize these facilities for Little League baseball, inter and intra district adult competition in many sports, to provide international entertainment such as José Iturbi (the world renowned pianist), present dramatic plays and musicals, parades and fairs for the children, etc.

There was considerable home entertaining as there was no place to go outside the compound. Aramco wives took on the challenge of gourmet cooking and many were very successful. For the bachelor employee to be able to enjoy a real home cooked meal was a great and much appreciated form of hospitality not only from Americans but from Lebanese, Pakistani, Syrian, Iraqi, and other Middle Eastern employee friends as well. Part of the home entertainment atmosphere dealt with the serving of alcoholic beverages. In the early days, Aramco was allowed by the Saudi Government to import beer, wine and whiskey. An unfortunate incident occurred that resulted in this "perk" being terminated. As the supply of these beverages disappeared, enterprising engineers designed and had built distillation equipment to make alcohol from sugar, water and yeast. The pure alcohol (after dilution) was then flavored with gin drops, rum flavoring, or stored in charred oak kegs to become bourbon. Some people still preferred unflavored "white lightening" as the diluted pure ethyl alcohol was termed. There were attempts to make wine and beer which this writer feels were not too successful. The cardinal rule was do not supply these products to the Saudis and keep the activity confined to the home.

Workdays followed the Muslim calendar with Friday as the seventh day of rest. Initially, five and one-half eight hour days were worked per week. Later, the workdays were reduced to five only. Paid vacations occurred annually, and after one year, round trip travel costs for an employee and his dependents were covered to Beirut. After two years, round trip travel costs were covered to the employee's home base in the U.S. The vacation periods were two weeks after one year and three days per month of service after two years (for example, with 24 months of service in Saudi Arabia, the employee would accumulate 72 vacation days plus travel time). Occasionally, holidays and a weekend would afford the opportunity to make short trips to local points of interest in the area such as Bahrain, Lebanon, Egypt, Iran, Jordan etc. The generous vacation policy of Aramco provided the opportunity for its employees to travel throughout the world…to Asia, the Far East, Europe, and Africa. This ability to travel and living in an Arab country resulted in Aramco personnel and their families becoming more worldly, more tolerant and more understanding of other cultures particularly the Arab culture.

Aramco always endeavored to make the environment as pleasant as possible for its employees. Their radio station broadcast 24 hours per day with three frequencies for music in a popular vein, country western and classical.

My personal taped music collection still affords good listening compliments of Aramco. Christian religious services were permitted within the company districts once per month. The Saudi Government permitted a Protestant minister and a Catholic priest to enter the country and conduct services alternatively (on Friday), i.e. one weekend in Dhahran, the second in Ras Tanura and the third in Abqaiq. A local bank provided banking services in office facilities provided by Aramco in each district. Schooling through grade school (grades 1 – 8) on the American system was available in company built schools; teachers from the U.S. and the Middle East were recruited for the school system, just as any other employee. Medical facilities included hospitals in each community with the main hospital located in Dhahran. Only the most critical and complicated surgery was not performed, the company preferring to transport patients needing such surgery to Europe or to the U.S. Doctors and nurses were recruited from many locales: I personally received eye treatment from a Dutch doctor, a Saudi doctor performed hernia surgery and post treatment was received from Indian, Dutch, and Saudi nurses. A doctor neighbor even came to my rescue by prescribing treatment for my Kerry Blue Terrier dog when she suffered a urinary infection. Here is an example of how Aramcons pulled together to help each other (kind of similar to pioneer days in the U.S.).

The work was interesting and challenging, and there was never a time when there was a shortage of work. With pay scales that were very competitive to those in the U.S. and which were complemented by an overseas bonus and paid vacations, employees benefited financially. Aramco then was owned by four American oil companies: Standard Oil of California 30%, Texaco 30%, Standard (New Jersey) 30% and Socony Mobil 10%. These companies called upon Aramco to expand its oil production and refining facilities, and employment in Saudi Arabia reached a maximum in 1952 of 3,400 Americans, 6,000 foreign contract and 14,800 Saudis. Total levels diminished subsequently, except that the number of skilled Saudis increased dramatically primarily as a result of the company's ambitious and successful industrial training programs. The end result of dedicated training for the Saudis as well as the Government's sponsoring of advanced education for its best students has been their capability to take over the management and operation of the Arabian American Oil Company when it turned over the oil facilities to Saudi ownership and the company became Saudi Aramco.

This has been a brief attempt to tell readers a little bit about Aramco the company, life in Saudi Arabia and the Saudi people and other Arab people who I deeply respect. My 16 years in Saudi Arabia were a "lesson in life" that I will never forget and an experience that will live with me forever. The deep respect I have for them and their religion is a result of how they treated me. Working for Aramco is looked back upon as an honor and a privilege. My experiences working for that wonderful company and being able to benefit from so many advantages it afforded is something I will always cherish. The company allowed me to meet Arabs and other Muslim peoples from many countries, to learn something of their culture and history, and most importantly to appreciate their many fine qualities. I had the experience of a lifetime. As an annuitant, I am also privileged to receive "Aramco World", a magazine which provides a continuing insight into Arab/Muslim life, history, geography and culture. One of their issues dealt with the love of the pure Arabian horse by the Polish, its importation into Poland and their continued breeding of the line. My Polish born wife shows that issue with pride to visitors.

Annex 3

A. CONTRACTING LECTURE

Polytechnic Institute, Lodz, Poland - October 2003

When I was invited to make a presentation on "Contracting" of lecture duration, my immediate reaction was one of dismay. How could I compress the many facets of the subject into this timeframe?

I quickly concluded that I could only talk about "highlights" or "major features" of the subject. I would not be able to go into the many details encompassed within the major scope of contracting.

This is what I have tried to do in my written presentation, which I understand you will be given copies of. Let me add, that like an author of a book, I had many "starts" to the paper before I gained the momentum to define the "highlights" of a broad and complex subject.

The Contracting written presentation included the following:

1. What is contracting?
2. The role of a contractor.
3. The principles of good contracting, including:

    a. Traps most often encountered.
    b. How to avoid the traps.

4. How good contracting is achieved.
5. The need for enforcement of project controls.
6. The types of contracts used, and:
7. Typical contracting activities, including an:

a. Emphasis on invitation to bid documentation to adequately define the work to be accomplished.

b. Emphasis on bid assessment to determine "soft money" or cost effects quantification for project execution.

You all can read the paper, and I hope understand it. I trust that it has been written in a simple enough fashion. I would like now to deviate from the written paper and talk about some of my experiences on the Shell/Esso North Cormorant Project and a little bit about the Esso Odin Project (both offshore oil/gas development projects). This deviation will hopefully prove to be more interesting than the theoretical aspects of the written text. These practical experiences, I believe, will lend further credence to the written presentation and the lessons learned that it describes.

All Shell U.K. Exploration & Production (Shell Expro UK) projects were named after birds of the North Sea. The cormorant is defined in the dictionary as a bird of no commercial value . . . no "omen" was intended with this name, and in fact, the oil field is still producing.

North Cormorant was the first joint venture offshore development by Shell Expro and Esso U.K. Exploration & Production (Esso Expro UK). One ongoing project at the time of North Cormorant was totally Shell Expro initiated and controlled.

From inception, i.e. seismic activities and exploratory drilling, to first oil production, the North Cormorant Project covered about a ten (10) year time-span. It was the first totally successful North Sea project, i.e. it was completed on schedule, final cost was within budget ($460 million were expended versus $600 million budgeted), and it met all safety criteria imposed by the U.K. government for offshore facilities installed in its territorial waters.

The project was conceived to produce 150,000 BPD (barrels per day) of oil from the U.K. sector of the North Sea, north of the Shetland Islands. This is a very "harsh" environment! The "weather window" for offshore installation activities only allows four (4) months of work time onsite per year. Once in production, of course, oil was flowing from the offshore platform twenty-four (24) hours per day except during downtime for maintenance.

Oil would be drilled for and produced from a single steel platform or "jacket" located strategically over the field and positioned in 540 feet of water depth (equivalent to 165 meters). Directional drilling would be used to reach the outermost and more central areas of the oil reservoir from the jacket. Typically, oil reservoirs are elongated, i.e. they are usually much longer than they are wide. From a single jacket then, only directional drilling would allow the extreme areas to be reached.

To give you some understanding of the North Cormorant jacket and what is under the water, presented now as Exhibit 1 attached is a picture of the plastic model built for fabrication planning purposes. The model represents 17,000 tons of steel fabrication.

- The jacket is anchored to the sea floor by piles (shown in blue) which are driven into the sea floor. They are positioned in clusters around the four (4) main legs of the jacket. It appears that there are eight (8) or nine (9) clustered piles around each leg.
- The piles are driven from the jacket through strategically located "pile guides . . . these are shown in gray.
- Notice the pronounced curvature of eighteen (18) flowlines (shown in orange) directionally drilled from the jacket and delivering oil and gas to the jacket from the remote areas of the reservoir. The other sixteen (16) flowlines, also directionally drilled access lesser remote areas of the reservoir.
- At the top, on each of the more narrow sides of the jacket are two (2) sets of three (3) "buoyancy tubes" filled with air. These are used to upright the jacket after it slides from a barge into the sea. If you can, imagine this huge structure weighing 17,000 tons rocking back and forth in the sea while it seeks to upright itself into a vertical position.
- The buoyancy tubes are later cut off once the jacket is fixed in place.
- The very thin line near the top of the jacket represents the water level.

The jacket model was also used for offloading tests simulating actual offshore conditions. These tests were performed by Delft University in Holland at their research facilities. In a huge specially designed water basin with tidal motion duplicated, the jacket model was pushed from a model barge into the water. Its buoyancy action was observed, recorded and analyzed to determine if its movements were satisfactory and predicting actual offshore motion of the jacket.

As a joint venture development by Shell Expro and Esso Expro, the North Cormorant Project was sanctioned to be self-governing, it had the responsibility of making its own decisions. It had the responsibility to hire its own personnel and procure the project's materials and equipment, and was remote from and only dealt with Shell/Esso management on major financial issues. Both companies provided a total of eleven (11) key project personnel.

From Esso: Project Manager (American)
Engineering Manager (American)–acted as substitute Project Manager when necessary
Project Services Manager (German)
Computer Modeling Engineer (American)
Contracts Engineer (American)
Jacket Design Engineer (American)

Topsides Design Engineer (American)
From Shell: Purchasing Manager (British)
Topsides Project Engineer (Dutch)
Drill Rig Design Engineer (British)
Project Accountant (Scottish)

These key people likewise were given responsibility for their functions and were held accountable for them. All other project personnel came from outside resources such as consulting companies, employment agencies (termed "body shoppers" in the U.K.), etc. These personnel were hired directly by the project. The team was quite international . . .

In addition to the above, we had: New Zealanders, Australians, Canadians and Irish.

I had the good fortune to be chosen as Contracts Engineer and to head the contracting function, and I joined the team under formation in October 1976 in Shell Expro's London offices on the Thames. At the time of my joining the team, there were about forty (40) members including administrative and support personnel. The contracting staff grew initially from me alone to six (6) additional contracts engineers when the project reached the bidding and award phases of the project's fabrication efforts.

My first challenge on joining the team was to evaluate the form of contract used by Shell Expro on its earlier projects. Was the form really suitable for offshore design and fabrication work? Up to that time, Shell Expro's record had not been good . . . its projects historically were overrun in cost and late in meeting schedule. Perhaps the form of contract being used was part of the problem. This was a question being asked.

The form of contract used buy Shell Expro had been written by an association of U.K. offshore facilities fabrication companies, and its terms heavily favored they, the contractors. This was not a situation looked favorably upon by the Esso key personnel, however, the weaknesses of the Shell Expro form had to be established.

A detailed clause by clause review of the Shell Expro contract form established that the majority of rights within the contract were with the contractor. The decision making rights of the client were minimal. For example, there were no provisions for handling "changes" to the scope of work (and there always are changes). Each change then, either client requested or contractor suggested, required a negotiation to agree on the scope change, how the change would be performed, pricing to be used and cost effect and schedule impact. Such negotiations were not conducive to expediting work, they were time and manpower consuming, and changes handled this way were most cost beneficial to the contractor. In such a manner of pricing changes, a contractor will usually take advantage of the opportunity to recover costs at rates in excess of those used to determine his bid under competition.

The lesson here is that the original contract should include mechanisms for handling changes such that pricing for them is also obtained under competitive award conditions. It is also worth mentioning that frequent negotiations on changes can be the source of ill will between the parties of the contract.

Another lesson learned is: do not use a contractor generated form of contract.

An encumbrance associated with the Shell Expro form of contract was that it required quantity measurement by quantity surveyors to determine progress. The quantity surveyors physically measured work progress compared to design drawings (a time consuming technique). In addition, the use of quantity surveyors imposed an added burden in contracting for their services, along with the extra costs for these services in the form of additional project manpower.

The Project Manager then made the decision that his project would impose and be run by the "Golden Rule", i.e." the guy with the gold rules" and that new contract forms were needed for the project and would be prepared.

As luck would have it, the eventual main source of contracts engineers available to the project was quantity surveyor (QS) companies. The quantity surveyors hired then required indoctrination into their first time use of Esso contract forms and would, on occasion, like to express their preference for a QS type of contract, however, they quickly adapted and were found to perform exceptionally well and to comment favorably on the quality of the Esso forms.

My next task then was to prepare a whole series of basic contract forms to be used by the project. These various forms are discussed in the written presentation. A "contracting" plan for the project was also prepared which dictated that all conceptual design and detailed design engineering contracts were to be reimbursable cost with a fixed fee, and all major fabrication contracts were to be lump sum (fixed price).

The subject of contract forms to be used provides a good example of how complexity of the forms did not permit me to go into details of their construction and many features in the written presentation. The reimbursable cost (RC) form developed for detailed design contracts was approximately seventy (70) pages excluding exhibits, and the lump sum (LS) form for fabrication contracts was approximately eighty (80) pages excluding exhibits. I could easily use an hour for each of these contract forms to discuss them in detail.

I might add that these forms were structured to provide maximum protection for Shell/Esso. Both the RC and the LS forms provided mechanisms for readily dealing with changes to the scope of work, as well as many client control/decision making features missing from the original Shell basic contract form.

The forms were not generated "out of the air" but were developed from basic Esso forms that were project proven but not on an offshore oil development project. The basic Esso forms therefore had to be "tailored" to a new environment of project activities. The "milestones" feature that was incorporated is discussed in the written presentation, and basically it provides an incentive to the contractor to complete a prescribed amount of work accomplishment. He is paid only after achieving the prescribed work of the milestone, be it a portion of the fixed fee in the RC contract or a portion of the lump sum in the LS contract. A project team representative is responsible for assuring completion of a milestone and approving payment for its achievement.

Initial reaction to the "milestones" concept by contractors was one of rejection. The contractors preferred financing early or progress payments tied to schedule. However, the North Cormorant team held firm in these situations, alternative payment proposals in bids by the contractors were rejected, and they were required to bid in compliance with the concept. Although the concept requires a degree of financing burden on the contractor (thus in his bid), the incentive to complete is believed more significant, i.e. beneficial to the project's achievement of schedule.

Project policy dictated the use of competition wherever possible. There would be no more of the "good old boy approach" where contracts were repeatedly awarded to the same "good old boy" because he had been used before and was a friend. This practice only breeds price inflation by the contractor. An example: offshore installation in the North Sea requires a dedicated monitoring of structural design, adherence to safety codes, procedural safety, fabrication procedures and installation procedures by a recognized quality assurance contractor. Shell Expro historically used Noble Denton, a U.K. company. The North Cormorant Project invited Det Norske Veritas of Norway into the bidding competition. Det Norske Veritas won the award with a lower bid by $150,000 and thus a saving to the project.

As the project team was being formed, a problem in fulfilling workday hours by Shell Expro personnel and its agency personnel was encountered. These employees were accustomed to a "perks" atmosphere of very relaxed employment: arrive late, leave early, long lunch breaks with cocktails and drinks in each of the Shell Expro offices on the Thames, and they were even able to take advantage of free full course meals offered for lunch time. One employee commuted by train from Southampton to London (approximately 1.5 hours) arriving at work about 0930 hours, was known to enjoy long liquid lunches, and departed the office about 1530 hours. The Project Manager tolerated this situation for a few weeks but then acted to enforce the office hours of a 0800 start, one (1) hour for lunch and a 1630 hours finish. The offenders were given a stern lecture on what was expected of them. A potential project team productivity problem was averted.

One might expect that there was all "smooth sailing" in the joint venture project management team. NOT SO! Initially, Esso people encountered strong resentment from the Shell Expro people to the new form of management being imposed upon them as well as the obvious control in the hands of the Esso majority. They resented being told how things were to be done . . . the Esso way. My main adversary in the beginning was the Project Accountant who loved to take exception to my every strategy. However, after my detailed analysis of the Shell Expro contract form was tabled, and the obvious benefits from competition began to be apparent, his adversity subsided. Then too, perhaps he was told by the Project Manager to become less "anti" and more cooperative, or else.

Competition remained the key in awarding contracts . . . the only major contracts that were not awarded under competition were those used for the conceptual designs, which preceded the detailed designs of the jacket, topsides facilities, drilling rig and a few smaller contracts. Here, the North Cormorant Project engaged consulting firms who had unique experience in these areas, and they were considered appropriate for "sole source" contracting, i.e. only one contractor is invited to bid. Even on these contracts, RC bids were solicited formally, and commercial terms were negotiated to the project's benefit. For example, if manpower rates or overheads were considered to be inflated, they would be negotiated lower.

Another element of competition was introduced to Shell Expro. Historically, Shell engaged consulting firms and "body shop" companies as a source of manpower. These companies quoted "all-in" rates for the services of their personnel offered to a project. An "all-in" rate is composed of the employee's wage, the company's overheads and a profit element. These "all-in" rates were never challenged by Shell Expro but were just accepted. An investigation of such companies revealed that some were charging as high as three (3) times the wage rate actually paid the employee being provided. By Esso standards, such an inflation constituted excessive profits and unrealistic overheads to the service provider. In the case of overheads, many "body shoppers" operated from a one-room rented office or from home with a card deck file and telephone, i.e. they had very little overheads.

Employment of outside personnel for the project was also a major and continuing activity. Upwards of nearly 500 personnel contracts were placed by the project's end. The savings to the project from less inflated "all-in" rates were never quantified to my knowledge, but directionally it must have helped the project's budget performance since the majority of team personnel always came from outside resources.

For conceptual design and major detailed design engineering contracts, bidders were required to quote and support (document) their overhead costs that would be billed to the project. Rejection of inflated overheads and their negotiation was commonplace.

The project was run from a computer generated network logic diagram. The computer model was a dynamic tool, constantly changing with every impact to the project either favorable or unfavorable. These impacts were incorporated into the model and thus reflected any effect on the project's cost and schedule. With this concept and the tool, the project status was always current and the project was under control. To build the model was a major task with each and every project key person and function involved. Each and every activity envisaged had to be assessed for cost-time-resources and recorded on a CTR form. For example, in my function, every contract anticipated had its own network activity diagram with CTR assessment for each activity in that diagram. These activities and their sequencing were incorporated into the overall project's cost and schedule model. This same procedure then was conducted by all project functions along with periodic updates for the function's activities.

To give you some understanding of the major contracting effort for the North Cormorant Project, Exhibit 2 (a simplified viewgraph of the jacket and topsides facilities) is presented. Depicted are: the jacket, the sub-deck which is positioned on top of the jacket and which houses the thirty-four (34) wellheads or "Christmas Trees" as they are known as. Then, the various topside facilities which sit on top of the sub-desk are shown including the process module (for separation of oil and gas) and the utilities module for combustion of gas (by combustion gas turbine) and power generation. The helideck is positioned on top of the living quarters. Also shown are the crane and flare modules.

The contract summary depicts the number of major contracts . . . there is one correction here: the crane and flare were fabricated under one (1) contract. You will note that there are six (6) major engineering contracts, seven (7) major onshore fabrication contracts one major offshore installation contract, and seven-eight (7-8) other offshore installation contracts. All of these major contracts were awarded under competition. In some cases, only two (2) bidders might be available, however, in most cases three-four (3-4) competitors were invited to bid. This contracting activity is mentioned here to emphasize the magnitude of such activities, since each bidding contractor's office and/or fabrication site was visited by a bid review team to evaluate the contractor's capacity for the work, the quality of his key personnel, his systems, his facilities/equipment, his commercial bid terms and his contractual exceptions. The site visits were followed by preparation of a formal award recommendation to management. Typically, the bid review team consisted of at least two (2) technical personnel and two (2) commercial personnel.

Of special interest, you will note only one (1) offshore installation contract. This type of work is very specialized, and it requires huge, seagoing, submersible, self-propelled installation vessels. Contractor availability at the time of the North Cormorant Project was limited to Heerema (Holland) and McDermott (U.S.A.). Only they had the type of installation vessels required. However, Heerema's vessel the "Balder" was the newest and state of the art, and they won the contract. Incidentally, the deck of the Balder is larger than a football (soccer) field with three (3) cranes of varying lifts up to thirty (30) tons. A second similar size vessel was then under construction by Heerema.

With a "weather window" of only four (4) months at the North Cormorant jacket location, and the limited availability of offshore installation contractors, an early contracting activity for such services was essential. The award to Heerema took place more than two (2) years prior to their actual work being undertaken.

The topsides detailed engineering design contract was bid by four (4) competitors. It excluded the drilling rig and the living quarters + helideck modules. A joint venture company of Taywood-Santa Fe won the contract based upon their fixed fee, reimbursable costs and a judgmental evaluation of their project execution capabilities (soft money). The joint venture was formed because neither partner could bring all the needed resources/facilities/expertise alone. Work was undertaken at dual office locations rendering coordination problems of the work and remote project team monitoring from the Shell Expro office. After about three (3) months, it became apparent that the topsides detailed design schedule was slipping and that design quality was unsatisfactory. Efforts to correct the trend had been unsuccessful, and the computer model predicted that the oil production date was in jeopardy. The design contract with Taywood-Santa Fe was terminated, and a new contract was awarded to Humphries & Glasgow, one of the original bidders and an established U.K. offshore design contractor with sufficient manpower and expertise under one (1) roof in their London offices. The North Cormorant team was moved into their offices, and the move was instrumental in turning the design effort back on schedule. Humphries & Glasgow had been the #2 bidder in the competition. The lesson learned here was that the bid evaluation effort was not satisfactory. It had not adequately assessed the negative impacts of a joint venture candidate, i.e. "soft money" costs for inadequate resources, dual office locations, previous offshore design experience, coordination procedures, etc. The joint venture low bid should have been debited to include greater "soft money" costs and thus exceeding the bid of the #2 ranked bidder. The result would have reversed the contractor selection.

The jacket detailed design, the living quarters-helideck detailed design and the drilling rig detailed design did not pose similar problems.

All of the fabrication contracts for these facilities were awarded with their detailed designs at least eighty-five (85) percent complete. This concept minimized changes to their scopes of work. No schedule delays were encountered on these contracts, and there were minimal claims activities resulting.

Of interest was the bidding for the jacket fabrication. Three contractors were invited to bid: one (1) French, one (1) American and one (1) Norwegian. The French company U.I.E. won the award with the lowest lump sum bid. However, in addition, it proposed dedicated services of a very strong project manager candidate. His experience and performance record on other jacket fabrications by U.I.E. was outstanding. A personal interview (as part of the bid review) confirmed his know-how, his abilities and his positive (take control) attitude required in managing a complex fabrication project. The lump sum contract form developed for the project, incidentally, incorporated a requirement that key personnel (such as the project manager) be dedicated to the project and that they could not be replaced without approval by the North Cormorant Project. The bid review team agreed that had U.I.E.'s bid not been the lowest, its recommendation for award would still have been U.I.E. because of its project manager candidate. The lesson here is that award to the lowest bidder may not always be the most prudent strategy.

By the time the project had reached the fabrication stage, the total project manpower had grown to about 550 people including site engineers and monitoring personnel at each of the fabrication sites. The fabrication sites were:

Jacket: France Process Module: U.K.

Sub-deck: U.K.Drill Rig Module: U.K.

Utilities Module: Holland Flare/Crane Module: U.K.

Living Quarters + Helideck Module: Holland

Offshore installation and offshore hookup and commissioning of facilities contracts were written as a combination of fixed fees and schedule of rates appropriate to the nature of the work . . . all of it being offshore, subject to weather, supply problems, etc. This is a unique type of contract, and time does not permit its discussion here.

The outstanding successes of the North Cormorant project were later enshrined in a project manual prepared by Shell Expro for its project personnel and for future projects. This manual put into writing all the "how to do it" concepts, procedures and techniques utilized by the North Cormorant Project including the types of contract forms developed for the project.

I might add that many of the good lessons learned on the North Cormorant Project were not carried over to my next assignment as Contracts Engineer on Esso Expro Norway's Odin Project in Stavanger, Norway.

That project to recover 200 MMSCFD of gas from the Norwegian sector of the North Sea was entirely staffed by key Esso personnel most of whom had never been associated with a project before. These personnel and responsible management were not receptive to and rejected recommendations based on "lessons learned", such as:

- Placing key personnel in the detailed design engineering contractor's office. The Odin Project attempted to monitor its topsides design contractor in London remotely from Stavanger. Control was quickly lost, and the contractor's design schedule slipped.
- To makeup schedule for lost design time, fabrication contracts were awarded prematurely, well before eighty-five (85) percent design completion.
- The prime topsides facilities fabrication contract was awarded with design approximately fifty (50) percent complete. The result of this imprudent strategy was extensive scope of work changes, schedule delay and a plague of contractor claims against the project which continued well after completion of the fabrication work.
- A computerized model of the project was not utilized to control the project. Hence, control rested with the contractor employed and not the project team.
- The project team was also hampered (restricted) by extensive political pressure, i.e. to award to Norwegian contractors. In one instance, the bid review team for the topsides process and utilities modules fabrication spent one and a half (1.5) weeks visiting U.K., Dutch, French and Norwegian bidders. The outcome of these visits and the resultant bid evaluation was a recommendation to award the contract to the Dutch bidder, being lowest in cost and judged best in meeting schedule and in work performance. This recommendation was ignored, and Esso Expro Norway management dictated that the award go to the Norwegian contender. The results of this decision added to the Odin Project's topside facilities fabrication problems just discussed above.
- When I expressed disbelief at this decision to the Project Services Manager by saying "I don't believe it" (i.e. because of the obvious waste of time, waste of manpower and costs to the project), he responded with "You better believe it". This exchange constituted one of our famous Contracting Mottos, some of which are included at the end of the written presentation.
- Because of the lack of experience of key project team members, control "by committee" tended to materialize. For example, the North Cormorant's proven project contract forms then being used for the Odin project were subjected to review by other team functions . . . the activity blessed by the Project Manager. This practice, both time consuming and manpower wasteful was eventually terminated upon strong objections of this presenter, believing very firmly in delegating responsibility for a project function.

That concludes my discussion of practical project experience on two (2) major North Sea oil/gas developments. The "lessons learned" are applicable to any type of project. Looking back, I consider my North Cormorant experience as the most rewarding of my career, and I would encourage any technically educated person to take advantage of an opportunity in project management.

B. CONTRACTING FOR PROJECTS

Contracting is not a "rocket science" . . . rather, it is a system of logical techniques and procedures coupled with principles of fairness. The system is aimed at optimizing the opportunities for achieving success of a project by a client buying the services of a contractor and at the same time affording the contractor the opportunity to earn a fair and reasonable profit for his services. This book provides a practical, useful and "hands-on" approach to the various contracting functions as follows including actual examples of what to do and what not to do. Throughout, it is written to highlight the most relevant and useful practices that should be considered when contracting for a project. The techniques and procedures to be utilized are applicable for major or minor projects, and the extent to which they are applied and the degree of detail utilized must be judged by the user.

Contract Forms

The maximum protection for a client buying the services of a contractor is afforded by the binding form of contract (including its supporting documentation) between the two parties. The various types of contract forms normally used, their composition and their applications are reviewed and discussed. Actual contract language is not included, as it would be too comprehensive and detailed for this text. Instead, the most important and critical clauses for a client's protection are recommended and discussed. As part of the discussion on contract composition, the basic concepts of reimbursable cost ("pay as you go") and lump sum ("fixed price"), and the type to use dependent upon the scope of work definition available is recommended. The degree of contract complexity desired for these concepts, depending upon the magnitude of project cost, is presented along with recommended contract types to be used for various project cost levels. Also, the different forms of payments under the reimbursable cost concept are reviewed along with suggested payment types for contract conditions encountered.

Supporting Contract Documentation

Depending upon the form of contract to be utilized (which is dependent upon the scope of work definition), the need for and importance of supporting documentation to the contract to define the contractor's scope of work and project responsibilities must be stressed repeatedly. Of necessity, a contractor invited to bid (or tender) on a lump sum basis, where he is taking on the maximum financial risk in performing the scope of work, should be provided with a detailed definition of that scope of work. Conversely, a contractor invited to bid on a reimbursable cost basis has a minimum financial risk as he is reimbursed for his costs and profit elements as the project proceeds and they occur. Thus, a less well-defined scope of work may be utilized.

Scope of Work

The magnitude and details of supporting documentation required for either a lump sum or reimbursable cost concept are analyzed and recommendations are made for the extent of engineering drawings, material lists, engineering standard drawings, etc. The necessity of compliance with municipal, state and country technical codes is most important.

Coordination Procedures

In achievement of a project, there are many phases of work required of a contractor dealing with the relationships between the parties of the contract. The need to define these phases of work and responsibilities are emphasized. Coordination Procedures are employed to define these responsibilities, and they usually include organization definition, project documentation quantification, reporting requirements, cost control procedures, schedule control procedures, inspection requirements, quality assurance and quality control requirements, invoicing procedures, accounting procedures, etc.

Screening

The technique of screening contractors to assess their availability and capability to perform and accomplish the work is outlined. The screening exercise is carried out prior to issuance of invitations to bid (tender), and it is intended to minimize the number of bidders to be invited to bid and thus afford the final contract bidders the most opportunity of winning the contract award. Three to four is suggested as a reasonable number of bidders, unless contractor availability is limited or when contractor required expertise is limited. A reduced number of bidders also minimizes the client's bid review activities. Screening, of necessity, should be directed at a broad number of contractors if possible. The questions to be asked of the contractors are outlined in detail, and from their responses, the potential bidders list to be invited can be developed. From the assessment of screening replies, the goal of obtaining competent, capable and viable project dedicated contractors can be achieved. Assessment and conclusions to be drawn from screening replies are discussed and reviewed.

Bidding

The elements of the formal invitation to bid documents are recommended. The details of these documents will be dependent upon the cost magnitude and scope of work for the project. The documents should include:

1. Invitation to Bid - a formal invitation which defines the schedule for bid submittal
2. Bid Submittal Form - ensures that all contractors submit their bids on the same basis
3. Form of Contract - the client's intended binding document
4. Scope of Work
5. Coordination Procedures

The bid submittal form is discussed with the intent of providing the client the opportunity to restrict the bidders from taking any exceptions to the bid documents or to permit the bidders to take exceptions to the bid documents. Since contractors will usually have exceptions to the bid documents, an opportunity for them to take exceptions is recommended for use, since technically, there can be improvements that a contractor's expertise may disclose which can improve the potential success of the project and the final quality of the product. Bid document exceptions may have cost and schedule impacts which should be quantified. Whatever exceptions are considered and approved, their negotiation and inclusion into the document involved must be achieved before final contract award. As part of a contractor's bid, his detailed project execution plan to accomplish the work is also required. The required elements of a project execution plan are reviewed and discussed. The bid submittal form should require the signature of a corporate officer of the contractor to ensure responsibility for the bid.

Bid Evaluation

The technique of a dedicated bid review team to evaluate contractor's bids is recommended. The team should consist of client's personnel qualified and capable of evaluating the commercial and contractual portions of the bids and the technical portions of the bids. These personnel should be allowed to perform their bid review assignments on a dedicated basis, that is, free from any other responsibilities while engaged in the bid review. Their dedication to bid review only is compatible with the usual urgency encountered in projects to achieve contract award and to commence the work. The two types of evaluations (commercial – technical) are suggested to be exclusive from each other to avoid any decision influences by the bid personnel. Only during the preparation of the final bid award recommendation should the personnel come together to establish the bases for award and to document it.

Strongly recommended, as part of the commercial terms analysis, is not only an assessment of the "hard money" portions of a contractor's bid which are directly defined or readily calculable from bid information but also an assessment of the "soft money" aspects of a contractor's bid which are not readily apparent. The types of "soft money" effects (which can only be estimated) may have a pronounced impact either positive or negative on cost and/or schedule for the project. An apparently low or best bid may be negated by consideration of "soft money" impacts. The types of these impacts, their methods of assessment, and potential conclusions from them are discussed and reviewed.

Final Contract

Only after all commercial, technical and contract terms have been agreed by both parties can the contract be signed. Negotiations during the bid review and right up to final contract signing may occur, and results of these negotiations should be documented precisely and incorporated into the contract documentation. The goal should be to ensure that there are no "loose ends" that later allow the contractor to request "changes to the scope of work" or eventual claims against the client. It is important to remember that a contractor's pricing for work is always less expensive while under competitive conditions than after award of the contract.

Selected Bibliography

Norman Boehm, Letter, "Balancing U.S. budget should be mandated", "Wilmington News Journal", March 23, 1994

Norman Boehm, Letter, "Oil Companies get ignorant criticism", "Wilmington News Journal", May 13, 2001

Norman Boehm, "Arabia nafta pachnaca. Z firma Aramco w sina dal", "Nowy Dziennik/ Weekend", October 18, 2003, New York, pp. 10-11

Norman Boehm, "Firma Aramco", "Teraz", Philadelphia, March 2004, pp. 18-20

Norman Boehm, "Bachelor Days", "Al-Ayyam Al-Jamilah", Winter 2002, pp. 24-27

Norman Boehm, "A North Dakota Welcome", "Alumni Review. University of North Dakota", November/December 2000, pp. 11-12

Norman Boehm, "Memories of UND", "Alumni Review. University of North Dakota", January/February 2003. pp. 18

Norman Boehm, "Alumni Days", Grand Forks, ND, May 25-25, 2005, pp. 11

"Bergman Book has Aramco Connection", Al-Ayyam Al-Jamilah", Spring 2014, pp. 4-5

Jan Nowak Jeziorański, "Polska droga do NATO" (Poland's Road to NATO), Tow. Przyjaciół Ossolineum, Wrocław 2006, ISBN 83-7095-079-5, pp. 16, 404, 405, 504, 526, Biogram, p. 592

Zmarl Norman Boehm, wielki przyjaciel Polski, Anna Bernat, PAP, "Dzieje PL Portal historyczny", June 17, 2016; "Polish Daily News", "Dziennik Zwiazkowy", Chicago June 18, 2016; "Veteran", montly by Polish Army Veterans Ass'n of America Inc., New York, July 2016

Barbara Henkel, "Bezpieczne zwiazki. Zwierzenia slawnych par", Warszawa 2003, ISBN 83-7386-046-0

Aleksandra Ziolkowska-Boehm, "Ingrid Bergman prywatnie" (Ingrid Bergman In Private), Proszynski, Warszawa, 2013, ISBN 978-83-7839-518-8

Aleksandra Ziolkowska-Boehm, "Ingrid Bergman and Her American Relatives", Hamilton Books, Lanham, MD, 2013, ISBN 978-0-7618-6150-8

Aleksandra Ziolkowska-Boehm, "Podróże z moją kotką" (Travels with My Cat); Warsaw 2002, 2004, ISBN 83-88576-90-9; ISBN 83-7386-102-5

Aleksandra Ziolkowska-Boehm, "On the Road with Suzy From Cat to Companion", Purdue University Press, West Lafayette, Indiana, 2010, ISBN 978-1-55753-554-2

Aleksandra Ziolkowska-Boehm, "Open Wounds – A Native American Heritage", Nemsi Books, Pierpont, SD, 2009, ISBN 978-0-9821427-5-2

Aleksandra Ziolkowska-Boehm, "Otwarta rana Ameryki" (America's Open Wound), Debit, Bielsko Biała 2007, ISBN 978-83-7167-556-0

Aleksandra Ziolkowska-Boehm, „Ulica Żółwiego Strumienia" (*Turtle Creek Boulevard*); Dom Ksiazki, Warsaw 1995, Wyd. Twoj Styl 2004, ISBN 83-900358-5-5, ISBN 83-7163-263-0

Aleksandra Ziolkowska-Boehm, "Love for Family, Friends, and Books", Hamilton Books, Lanham, MD, 2015, ISBN 978-0-7618-6568-1

Index